Logics for New-Generation AI
Second International Workshop
10-12 June 2022, Zhuhai

Volume 1
Proceedings of the First International Workshop, Hangzhou, 2021
Beishui Liao, Jieting Luo and Leendert van der Torre, eds

Volume 2
Proceedings of the Second International Workshop, Zhuhai, 2022
Beishui Liao, Réka Markovich and Yì N. Wáng, eds

Logics for New-Generation AI
Second International Workshop
10-12 June 2021, Zhuhai

Edited by

Beishui Liao
Réka Markovich
Yì N. Wáng

© Individual author and College Publications 2022
All rights reserved.

ISBN 978-1-84890-406-4

College Publications, London
Scientific Director: Dov Gabbay
Managing Director: Jane Spurr

http://www.collegepublications.co.uk

Original cover design by Laraine Welch

Preface

The First International Workshop on Logics for New-Generation Artificial Intelligence (LNGAI 2021) was successfully held in Hangzhou last year. The series of workshops are sponsored by the national key project "Research on Logics for New Generation Artificial Intelligence" (2021–2025). The topics of LNGAI involves five main research directions. They are non-monotonic logics and formal argumentation, which consist of logical foundations for dealing with incomplete, uncertain, dynamic and conflicting information in an open, dynamic and real environment, and three important applied areas of logical research: causal reasoning, reasoning with norms and values, and knowledge graph reasoning, which play indispensable roles in explainable AI, ethical AI and knowledge-based AI respectively. As an annual event, LNGAI 2022, the second workshop in the seires, is held at the Zhuhai Campus of Sun Yat-sen University, China, 10–12 June 2022.

In this workshop, we received 11 submissions. After rigorous peer-review by the international program committee, 7 long papers and 2 extended abstracts are accepted and included in this volume of proceedings. In addition, 5 abstracts from invited speakers of the workshop are also included in the proceedings. These papers and abstracts reflect very well the state-of-the-art of the research orientated to the above five research directions.

On one hand, concerning logical foundations for reasoning about incomplete, uncertain, dynamic and conflicting information, there are seven contributions in the directions of non-monotonic logics and formal argumentation. Chen Chen and Beishui Liao propose a framework which extends EAF with the strength of evidence and indicate that the strength of an argument is determined by the accumulation of evidences supporting the argument. David Fuenmayor and Christoph Benzmüller propose a technique of shallow semantical embeddings of non-classical logics in higher-order logic, allowing the logico-pluralist formalization of arguments and their dialectical interactions. Puyin Li et al introduce a weighted quantitative argumentation framework based on regression, which is a further extension of the model proposed by Pietro Baroni. Henry Prakken (invited speaker) argues that the principle-based approach applied to evaluate formal argumentation semantics may not be very principled and takes gradual semantics for illustration. Muyun Shao and Beishui

i

Liao propose a model of multi-agent control game and study how agents adjust their strategies and form coalitions in reaction to unforeseeable changes of the environment. Christian Straßer (invited speaker) introduces some recent developments in the argumentative unification of defeasible reasoning. Xuefeng Wen proposes a new set of axiomatizations for Lewis' conditional logics, without using CSO, or RCEA, or the rule of interchange of logical equivalents.

On the other hand, about the logical models and algorithms adopted in explainable AI, ethical AI and knowledge-based AI, there are also seven contributions. J.-Martín Castro-Manzano proposes a synthetic term logic by mixing four logics which are designed to capture four aspects of natural language reasoning, namely assertion, numeracy, modality and relevance. Huajun Chen (invited speaker) provides a structured overview of new trends of neural-symbolic methods from perspectives of new developments of the knowledge graphs and deep neural networks. Ali Farjami adopts LogiKEy to experiment and compare Åqvist preference models with Kratzer models for conditional obligations. Xiaolong Liang and Yì N. Wáng introduce weighted graphs and as a special case of it, similarity graphs, which can be used to model similarity between epistemic objects. Yongmei Liu (invited speaker) introduces her recent work on multi-agent epistemic planning based on higher-order belief change, and the ongoing work on a model-theoretic definition of higher-order belief revision and its syntactic characterizations. Valeria de Paiva (invited speaker) introduces the task of Natural Language Inference is to test whether the system can detect entailment, contradiction, or neutrality between pairs of sentences. Alexander Sakharov investigates logical foundations of the derivation of literals from non-Horn knowledge bases with fuzzy predicates.

We would like to thank the invited speakers and the authors for their contributions to the workshop. Thanks to the program committee – Michael Anderson, Pietro Baroni, Christoph Benzmüller, Alexander Bochman, Dragan Doder, Huimin Dong, Kun Kuang, John-Jules Meyer, Gabriella Pigozzi, Tjitze Rienstra, Olivier Roy, Guillermo Simari, Chenwei Shi, Leon van der Torre and Bin Wei – for their careful reviews of the submissions. Meanwhile, we want to thank local organizers Huimin Dong and Xiaolong Liang from Sun Yat-sen University for their excellent work in organizing this event. Finally, we acknowledge the financial support on LNGAI 2022 from the Key Program of the National Social Science Foundation of China, No. 20&ZD047.

Beishui Liao, Réka Markovich & Yì N. Wáng
Zhejiang University, Hangzhou, China
University of Luxembourg, Luxembourg
Sun Yat-sen University, Zhuhai, China
June 3, 2022

Contents

Neural Symbolic Computing with Knowledge Graph

Huajun Chen

Zhejiang University, Hangzhou, P.R. China

Abstract

The combination of old-fashioned symbolic methods with artificial neural networks has a long-standing history, normally referred as so-called neural-symbolic methods. In this talk, we provide a structured overview of new trends of neural-symbolic methods from perspectives of new developments of the knowledge graphs and deep neural networks. The topic covers several subfields including embedding knowledge graphs with neural networks, pretraining large-scale knowledge graphs, injecting knowledge graphs into deep neural networks, etc.

Multi-Agent Epistemic Planning Based on Higher-Order Belief Change

Yongmei Liu

Sun Yat-sen University, Guangzhou, P.R. China

Abstract

In recent years, multi-agent epistemic planning has received attention from both dynamic logic and planning communities. Existing implementations of multi-agent epistemic planning are based on compilation into classical planning and suffer from various limitations. In this talk, I will introduce our recent work on multi-agent epistemic planning based on higher-order belief change, and our ongoing work on a model-theoretic definition of higher-order belief revision and its syntactic characterizations. We consider centralized multi-agent epistemic planning from the viewpoint of a third person who coordinates all the agents to achieve the goal. In our framework, the initial knowledge base (KB) and the goal, the preconditions and effects of actions can be arbitrary KD45n formulas, the solution is an action tree branching on sensing results, and the progression of KBs w.r.t. actions is achieved through the operation of belief revision or update on KD45n formulas, that is, higher-order belief revision or update. To support efficient reasoning and progression, we make use of a normal form for KD45n called alternating cover disjunctive formulas (ACDFs). To give a model-theoretic definition of higher-order belief revision, we propose a variant of Moss' canonical formulas which we call alternating canonical formulas, treat them as models and define distances between them.

Natural Language Inference: for Humans and Machines

Valeria de Paiva

Topos Institute, Berkeley, the United States

Abstract

One hears much about the incredible results of recent neural nets methods in Natural Language Processing (NLP). In particular much has been made of the results on the Natural Language Inference (NLI) task using the huge new corpora SNLI, MultiNLI, SciTail, etc, constructed since 2015. The main idea of the NLI task is that to test understanding of the language one checks whether the system can detect entailment, contradiction, or neutrality between pairs of sentences. Thus the sentence "John arrived" entails the sentence "A person arrived", contradicts the sentence "No one arrived" and it is neutral with respect to the sentence "John and Mary arrived", while the sentence "John and Mary arrived" entails "John arrived". Wanting to join in the fun of doing logic with sentences instead of formulae, we decided to check the results on the corpus SICK (Sentences Involving Compositional Knowledge), which is two orders of magnitude smaller than SLNI, but curated by linguists and hence presumably easier to deal with.

We discovered that there were many results that did not agree with our logical intuitions. As a result, we have written several papers on the subject of NLI on SICK. I want to show you a potted summary of this work, to explain why we think the work on NLI is not near completion, yet, despite claims that modern neural nets systems achieve superhuman performance on the existing benchmarks. I plan to also describe how we're tackling NLI, why we think this problem is very important and how we envisage the next steps.

Principle-Based and Principled Formal Studies of Argumentation: The case of gradual semantics

Henry Prakken

Utrecht University, Utrecht, Netherlands
University of Groningen, Netherlands
European University Institute, Florence, Italy

Abstract

In 2007, two papers of Baroni & Giacomin and Caminada & Amgoud introduced the idea of a principle-based approach to the study of formal argumentation semantics. In such an approach, a number of principles (also referred to as 'axioms', 'postulates' or 'properties') for argumentation semantics are formulated and then used to characterise or evaluate a given argumentation semantics. A principle-based approach can be purely mathematical in that it does not take a stance on whether the studied principles are desirable. However, principles can also be seen as rationality constraints on argument evaluation. An (often implicit) underlying idea is then that the more principles a semantics satisfies, the better it is.

This underlying idea is justified to the extent that the proposed principles are themselves justified. Ideally, the principles would be based on generally accepted philosophical insights about the modelled argumentation phenomena. However, often the principles are not justified in this way but instead appear to be based on the authors' intuitions.

In this talk I will argue that if the principle-based approach is applied in an intuition-driven way to evaluate semantics, it is not very principled. I will do so by discussing recent studies of gradual acceptability semantics. I will argue that such studies should distinguish between logical, dialectical and rhetorical argument strength, and I will propose a new definition of dialectical argument strength founded on philosophical insights.

Some Recent Developments in the Argumentative Unification of Defeasible Reasoning

Christian Straßer

Ruhr-University Bochum, Bochum, Germany

Abstract

In his seminal 1995 paper on abstract argumentation Dung envisioned formal argumentation as a unifying framework for defeasible reasoning. The latter has been modeled in its many facets in terms of nonmonotonic logic. The unifying power of formal argumentation is substantiated if central nonmonotonic methods can be naturally phrased as forms of argumentative reasoning.

In this talk I will highlight some recent developments along these lines. First, I will demonstrate how sub-classes of logic-based argumentation characterize Makinson's method of default assumptions and the family of adaptive logics (joint work with Ofer Arieli and AnneMarie Borg). Second, I will illustrate how Makinson and Van der Torre's nonmonotonic input-output logics can be characterized by sequent-based argumentation and an underlying elegant proof calculus (joint work with Kees van Berkel). These two results generalize previous characterizations of reasoning with maximal consistent sets in the tradition of Rescher and Manor. Finally, I will show how several classes of prioritized default logic can be characterized in terms of AS-PIC+, generalizing previous results by Liao et al (joint work with Pere Pardo).

On Mixing Term Logics

J.-Martín Castro-Manzano

UPAEP University
21 sur 1103, Puebla, Mexico

Abstract

In this contribution we try to mix four term logics as to produce a synthetic term logic. To reach this goal we briefly sketch four logics designed to capture four aspects of natural language reasoning—assertion, numeracy, modality, and relevance—and then we mix said logics in order to produce a synthetic logic together with a tableaux proof method.

Keywords: Tableaux, term logic, numerical logic, modal logic, relevant logic.

1 Introduction

Broadly speaking, the *raison d'être* of logic is the study of inference within natural language [20], and in order to study inference in this sense it is customary to use Fregean, first order languages [11,18,34,3,19]. However, even if this standard is common to us when teaching, researching, or applying logic—this is the received view of logic, after all (cf. [8])—, there is no need to be particularly acute in order to notice that this view of logic may indeed be familiar, but that does not make it natural [36,14,23,46,28,16].

Consequently, in an effort to deal with natural language reasoning, since the late 50's Sommers championed a revision of the traditional, Aristotelian term logic. His project unfolded into three branches—ontology, semantics, and logic (cf. [37])—that became, respectively, a theory of categories, a theory of truth, and a theory of logic known as Term Functor Logic [35,36,38,12,14,17].

This last theory is a plus-minus algebra that uses terms and functors rather than first order language elements such as variables or quantifiers (cfr. [32,30,24,36,37]). Following the tenets of this project, in this contribution we try to mix four term logics as to produce a synthetic term logic. To reach this goal we briefly sketch four logics designed to capture four aspects of natural language reasoning—assertion, numeracy, modality, and relevance—and then we mix said logics in order to produce a synthetic logic together with a tableaux proof method. At the end we discuss some of the features of this proposal.

2 Four Term logics

2.1 Assertoric term logic

Assertoric syllogistic—the logic at the core of traditional, Aristotelian term logic—is a term logic that makes good use of categorical statements in order to capture a basic notion of assertion. A categorical statement is a statement composed by two terms, a quantity, and a quality. Typically, we say a categorical statement is a statement of the form:

$$\langle Quantity \rangle \; \langle \mathsf{S} \rangle \; \langle Quality \rangle \; \langle \mathsf{P} \rangle$$

where $Quantity = \{All, \; Some\}$, $Quality = \{is, \; is \; not\}$, and S and P are term-schemes. From the standpoint of Sommers & Englebretsen's (assertoric) Term Functor Logic (TFL^α, from now on) [35,36,38,12,14,17], we say:

Definition 2.1 [Categorical statement in TFL^α] A categorical statement in TFL^α is a statement of the form:

$$\pm\mathsf{S} \pm \mathsf{P}$$

where $\pm$ are functors, and S and P are term-schemes.

So, for example, we can model the four traditional, categorical statements in TFL^α as follows, where the term L stands for *logicians*, and S stands for *smart*:[1]

Statement	TFL^α
All logicians are smart.	$-\mathsf{L} + \mathsf{S}$
No logician is smart (i.e. all logicians are not smart).	$-\mathsf{L} - \mathsf{S}$
Some logicians are smart.	$+\mathsf{L} + \mathsf{S}$
Some logicians are not smart.	$+\mathsf{L} - \mathsf{S}$

Table 1
Categorical statements in TFL^α.

Given this language (say, $\mathcal{L}_{\mathsf{TFL}^\alpha} = \langle \mathcal{T}, \pm \rangle$, where $\mathcal{T} = \{\mathsf{A}, \mathsf{B}, \mathsf{C}, \ldots\}$ is a set of terms, and $\pm$ is shorthand for the $+$ and $-$ functors), TFL^α offers a sense of validity as follows [14, p.167]:

---

[1] In this context, terms as those elements into which a statement can be divided, that is, into that which is predicated of something (i.e. the predicate) and that of which something is predicated (i.e. the subject), as Aristotle suggested (*Pr. An.* A1, 24b16–17); whereas functors are logical expressions. As [15] explains, a term might be formed by the use of a single word or a complex of words. In English, for example *smart*, and *logician*, are terms, as well, as *taught Plato*, or *in the agora* are terms. Terms are what the medieval scholastic philosophers called *categoremata*; whereas functors are *syncategoremata*, that is, words that are not terms but are used to turn terms into more complex terms. In English, for example, *and, or, only if, if ... then, all, some, not, is,* and *is not* are functors.

Definition 2.2 [Valid syllogism (in TFL^α)] A syllogism is valid (in TFL^α) iff:

(i) The algebraic sum of the premises is equal to the conclusion, and

(ii) the number of particular conclusions (*viz.*, zero or one) is equal to the number of particular premises. [2]

And so, with this logic we can model assertoric inferences like the one shown in Table 2.

	Statement	TFL^α
1.	All philosophers are smart.	$-P + S$
2.	All logicians are philosophers.	$-L + P$
⊢	All logicians are smart.	$-L + S$

Table 2
A valid assertoric inference.

2.2 Numerical term logic

Murphree's Numerical Term Logic (TFL^ν)—which serves as an extension of numerical syllogistic [43,44]—is a term logic that tries to capture numeracy by representing and performing inference with numerical quantifiers [29]. In this logic, a numerical statement is a statement of the form:

$$\langle Quantity \rangle \ \langle \mathsf{n} \rangle \ \langle \mathsf{S} \rangle \ \langle Quality \rangle \ \langle \mathsf{P} \rangle$$

where $Quantity = \{All, \ All \ but, \ At \ most, \ At \ least, \ More \ than, \ Some\}$, $\mathsf{n} \in \Re^+$, $Quality = \{is, \ is \ not\}$, and S and P are term-schemes. Formally, since TFL^ν is a conservative extension of TFL^α, we say:

Definition 2.3 [Numerical statement in TFL^ν] A numerical statement in TFL^ν is a statement of the form:

$$\pm_\mathsf{n} \mathsf{S} \pm \mathsf{P}$$

where $\pm$ are functors, $\mathsf{n} \in \Re^+$, and S and P are term-schemes.

---

[2] We must mention that this approach is not only capable of representing syllogistic inference, since it can also represent relational, singular, and compound statements with ease and clarity [12], but for our current purposes, this exposition will suffice.

Thus, we can model the four traditional, categorical statements in TFL^ν as follows:

Statement	TFL^ν
All logicians are smart.	
At most 0 logicians are not smart.	$-_0\mathsf{L}+_\mathsf{S}$
All but 0 logicians are smart.	
No logician is smart.	
At most 0 logicians are smart.	$-_0\mathsf{L}-\mathsf{S}$
All but 0 logicians are not smart.	
Some logicians are smart.	
More than 0 logicians are smart.	$+_1\mathsf{L}+\mathsf{S}$
At least 1 logician is smart.	
Some logicians are not smart.	
More than 0 logicians are not smart.	$+_1\mathsf{L}-\mathsf{S}$
At least 1 logician is not smart.	

Table 3
Categorical statements in TFL^ν.

Something similar happens with the generalization of these statements for $n > 0$, as follows: [3]

Statement	TFL^ν
At most n logicians are not smart.	$-_n\mathsf{L}+\mathsf{S}$
All but n logicians are smart.	
At most n logicians are smart.	$-_n\mathsf{L}-\mathsf{S}$
All but n logicians are not smart.	
More than n logicians are smart.	$+_n\mathsf{L}+\mathsf{S}$
At least n logicians are smart.	
More than n logicians are not smart.	$+_n\mathsf{L}-\mathsf{S}$
At least n logicians are not smart.	

Table 4
Numerical statements in TFL^ν.

Consequently, given this language ($\mathcal{L}_{\mathsf{TFL}^\nu} = \langle \mathcal{T}, \pm, \Re^+ \rangle$), TFL^ν offers the next notion of validity [29]:

---

[3] In these examples, the first expression is called *simple interpretation*), whereas the second is known as *exceptive interpretation* [40]. These interpretations are important and interesting because they help us represent exact quantifiers as follows:

- Exactly n S are P := $+(+_{n-1}\mathsf{S}+\mathsf{P})+(-_n\mathsf{S}+\mathsf{P})$

- Exactly n S are not P := $+(+_{n-1}\mathsf{S}-\mathsf{P})+(+_n\mathsf{S}+\mathsf{P})$

So, for instance, in order to represent the claim that there are exactly two smart logicians we could write $+(+_1\mathsf{L}+\mathsf{S})+(-_2\mathsf{L}+\mathsf{S})$, that is to say, more than one logician is smart and at most 2 logicians are smart. Additionally, given this account of exact quantification, comparative and fractional quantifiers only require some additional tweaks [40].

Definition 2.4 [Valid syllogism (in TFL$^\nu$)] A syllogism is valid (in TFL$^\nu$) iff:

(i) The algebraic sum of the premises is equal to the conclusion,

(ii) the number of particular conclusions (*viz.*, zero or one) is equal to the number of particular premises, and

(iii) either *(a)* the value of a universal conclusion (i.e. a conclusion that begins with a minus sign) is equal to the sum of the values of the universal premises, or *(b)* the value of a particular conclusion (i.e. a conclusion that begins with a plus sign) is equal to the difference of the universal premise minus the particular. [4]

Following our previous exposition pattern, and as an example, consider the inference shown in Table 5.

	Statement	TFL$^\nu$
1.	All but 11 philosophers are logicians.	$-_{11}P + L$
2.	At least 30 smart people are philosophers.	$+_{30}S + P$
⊢	At least 19 smart people are logicians.	$+_{19}S + L$

Table 5
A valid numerical inference.

2.3 Modal term logic

Englebretsen's Modal Term Functor Logic (TFL$^\mu$)—a formal version of modal syllogistic [1,2,27,25,22,21,39,13,33,42,26]—tries to capture modality by extending TFL$^\alpha$ with □ and ◇ [13,17]. So, given a term T, TFL$^\mu$ allows the next combinations: $+\Box + T$ (i.e. $\Box + T$), $+\Box - T$ (i.e. $\Box - T$), $-\Box + T$ (i.e. $-\Box T$), $-\Box - T$, and, as usual, the operator ◇ is defined as $-\Box-$. Thus, we can say a *de dicto* modal statement is a statement of the form:

$$\langle Modality \rangle \; (\langle Quantity \rangle \; \langle S \rangle \; \langle Quality \rangle \; \langle P \rangle);$$

and a *de re* modal statement is a statement of the form:

$$\langle Quantity \rangle \; \langle S \rangle \; \langle Quality \rangle \; \langle Modality \rangle \; \langle P \rangle$$

where $Modality = \{\diamond, \Box\}$, $Quantity = \{All, Some\}$, $Quality = \{is, \; is \; not\}$, and S and P are term-schemes. Thus, formally:

Definition 2.5 [Modal statement in TFL$^\mu$] A modal statement in TFL$^\mu$ is a statement of one of the following forms:

$$\mu(\pm S \pm P)|\pm S \pm P|\pm S \pm \mu P$$

where $\pm$ are functors, μ is a modality, and S and P are term-schemes.

So, for example, we can represent modal *de re*, *de dicto*, and combined statements in TFL$^\mu$ as follows:

---

[4] This last condition is different from Szabolcsi's Numerical Term Logic, which requires that the value of the premises need to be equal or greater than the value of the conclusion (cfr. [40]).

Statement	TFL$^\mu$
All logicians are (not) necessarily smart.	$-L \pm \Box S$
All logicians are (not) possibly smart.	$-L \pm \diamond S$
Some logicians are (not) necessarily smart.	$+L \pm \Box S$
Some logicians are (not) possibly smart.	$+L \pm \diamond S$
Necessarily all logicians are (not) smart	$\Box(-L \pm S)$
Possibly all logicians are (not) smart	$\diamond(-L \pm S)$
Necessarily some logicians are (not) smart	$\Box(+L \pm S)$
Possibly some logicians are (not) smart	$\diamond(+L \pm S)$
Necessarily all (some) logicians are (not) necessarily smart	$\Box(\pm L \pm \Box S)$
Necessarily all (some) logicians are (not) possibly smart	$\Box(\pm L \pm \diamond S)$
Possibly all (some) logicians are (not) necessarily smart	$\diamond(\pm L \pm \Box S)$
Possibly all (some) logicians are (not) possibly smart	$\diamond(\pm L \pm \diamond S)$

Table 6
Modal *de re*, *de dicto*, and combined statements in TFL$^\mu$.

Given this language ($\mathcal{L}_{\mathsf{TFL}^\mu} = \langle \mathcal{T}, \pm, \mathcal{M} \rangle$, where $\mathcal{M} = \{\diamond, \Box\}$), we have the next notion of validity [13,17]:

Definition 2.6 [Valid syllogism (in TFL$^\mu$)] A syllogism is valid (in TFL$^\mu$) iff:

(i) The algebraic sum of the premises is equal to the conclusion,

(ii) the number of particular conclusions (*viz.*, zero or one) is equal to the number of particular premises,

(iv) the conclusion is not stronger than any premise, [5] and

(v) the number of *de dicto*-$\diamond$ premises is not greater than the number of *de dicto*-$\diamond$ conclusions.

As an example, consider the inference shown in Table 7.

	Statement	TFL$^\mu$
1.	All philosophers are necessarily smart.	$-P + \Box S$
2.	All logicians are philosophers.	$-L + P$
$\vdash$	All logicians are necessarily smart.	$-L + \Box S$

Table 7
A valid modal inference.

2.4 Relevance term logic

Relevance Term Logic (TFL$^\rho$) is an extension of TFL$^\alpha$ that captures a notion of relevance by following some insights of the Aristotelian sense of causal rele-

---

[5] According to [13], there is a transitivity or "strength" of modal operators in such a way that $\Box T$ implies $T\Box$, $T\Box$ implies T, T implies $T\diamond$, and $T\diamond$ implies $\diamond T$. So, a first statement (or term) is stronger than a second statement (or term) if and only if the first entails the second but not the other way around. The intuition is that a necessary condition for the validity of any syllogism is that the conclusion cannot exceed any premise in strength: the scholastics called this the *peiorem* rule, namely, *peiorem semper sequiter conclusio partem*.

vance (cfr. [41,45]). It represents pieces of complex discourse (insofar as they include at least two premises and one conclusion) with mood and figure (because the order of statements and terms matters) in which a conclusion that is different from the premises (thus avoiding *petitio principii*) necessarily (and hence deductively) follows from and depends on said premises (thus avoiding irrelevance, *non causa ut causa*). In this logic we say a relevant statement is a statement of the form:

$$\langle Quantity \rangle \ \langle S \rangle \ \langle Quality \rangle \ \langle P \rangle \ \langle Flag \rangle$$

where $Quantity = \{All, \ Some\}$, $Quality = \{is, \ is \ not\}$, S and P are term-schemes, and $Flag = \{p_i, \ c\}$ for $i \in \{1, 2, 3, \ldots\}$ is a set of (premise or conclusion) flags. So, formally, we say:

Definition 2.7 [Relevant statement in TFL$^\rho$] A relevant statement in TFL$^\rho$ is a statement of the form:

$$\pm S \pm P_f$$

where $\pm$ are functors, S and P are term-schemes, and f is a flag.

Hence, for example, we can represent categorical statements in TFL$^\rho$ as follows:

Statement	TFL$^\rho$
All logicians are smart.	$-L + S_f$
No logician is smart (i.e. all logicians are not smart).	$-L - S_f$
Some logicians are smart.	$+L + S_f$
Some logicians are not smart.	$+L - S_f$

Table 8
Categorical statements in TFL$^\rho$.

With this language ($\mathcal{L}_{\mathsf{TFL}^\rho} = \langle \mathcal{T}, \pm, \mathcal{F} \rangle$, where $\mathcal{F}$ is a set of flags), TFL$^\rho$ offers a notion of validity as follows:

Definition 2.8 [Valid syllogism (in TFL$^\rho$)] A syllogism is valid (in TFL$^\rho$) iff:

(i) The algebraic sum of the premises is equal to the conclusion,

(ii) the number of particular conclusions (*viz.*, zero or one) is equal to the number of particular premises, and

(vi) all the flags of the premises are reclaimed for reaching the conclusion and the flags of the conclusion are different to the flags of the premises.

And so, with this logic we can model relevant inferences such as the one shown in Table 9. [6]

	Statement	TFL^ρ
1.	All philosophers are smart.	$-\mathsf{P} + \mathsf{S}_{p_1}$
2.	All logicians are philosophers.	$-\mathsf{L} + \mathsf{P}_{p_2}$
⊢	All logicians are smart.	$-\mathsf{L} + \mathsf{S}_c$

Table 9

A valid relevant inference.

2.5   Term logics tableaux

Now, given the previous exposition, one could think the notion of validity for these logics only covers monadic or syllogism-like inferences, but as we hinted in a previous note, that would be a hasty conclusion. Indeed, we can extend said notions of validity either by enlarging the rules of inference [12] or, following [10,31], by implementing tableaux proof methods [9,6,4,7,5]. So, if we let ϕ and ψ stand for arbitrary TFL well formed formulas, we can say an inference is valid namely, $\vdash -\phi + \psi$ iff ψ is obtained from ϕ by applying some adequate rule of inference or by following tableaux procedures. Here we focus on the latter.

Thus, as usual, we can say a *tableau* is an acyclic connected graph determined by nodes and vertices. The node at the top is called *root*. The nodes at the bottom are called *tips*. Any path from the root down a series of vertices is a *branch*. To test an inference for validity we construct a tableau which begins with a single branch at whose nodes occur the premises and the rejection of the conclusion: this is the *initial list*. We then apply the expansion rules that allow us to extend the initial list: consider Diagram 1.

---

[6] At this point, someone might wonder—and with good reason—what is the difference between the inference in Table 9 and the inference shown in Table 2, because they look all the same. And the answer to this question is precisely that: they are the same; but that is a virtue of the example (because it is a *bona fide* syllogism by design), not a vice of the logic. In order to illustrate this point consider, for sake of comparison, an irrelevant but truth-preserving inference, namely, a *petitio*:

	Statement	TFL^ρ
1.	All logicians are smart.	$-\mathsf{L} + \mathsf{S}_{p_1}$
⊢	All logicians are smart.	$-\mathsf{L} + \mathsf{S}_{p_1}$

Clearly, *petitio* is not a syllogism (because it has only one premise) and yet it complies with conditions (i) and (ii) of TFL^α, that is to say, it is valid in TFL^α but, surely, it cannot be causally relevant, for the premise is equal to the conclusion. Now, since Aristotelian relevance requires premises and conclusions to be disjoint (*Topics* 100a25-26, *De Sophisticis Elenchis* 165a1-2, *Pr. An.* 24b19-20, *Pos. An.* 1, III, 72b25-32), the use of flags allows us to determine that even if *petitio* is truth-preserving, it fails to meet condition (iii) for causal relevance: the flags of the conclusion are not different to the flags of the premises. A full discussion on this issue is given in another place.

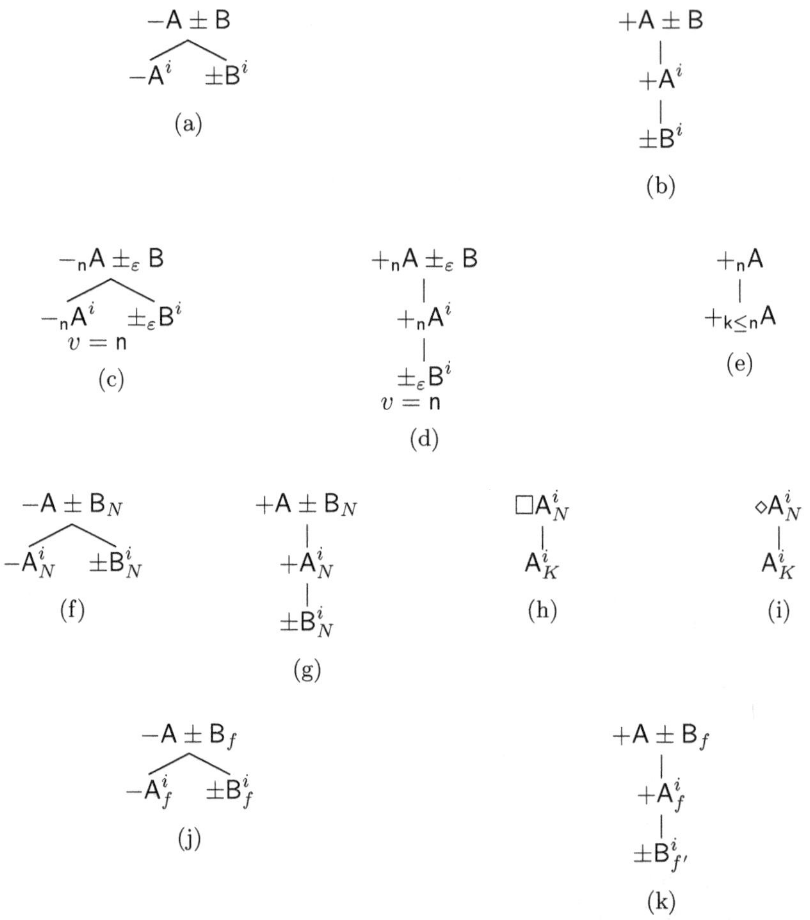

$$-A \pm B$$
$$-A^i \quad \pm B^i$$

(a)

$$+A \pm B$$
$$|$$
$$+A^i$$
$$|$$
$$\pm B^i$$

(b)

$$-_n A \pm_\varepsilon B$$
$$-_n A^i \quad \pm_\varepsilon B^i$$
$$v = n$$

(c)

$$+_n A \pm_\varepsilon B$$
$$|$$
$$+_n A^i$$
$$|$$
$$\pm_\varepsilon B^i$$
$$v = n$$

(d)

$$+_n A$$
$$|$$
$$+_{k \leq n} A$$

(e)

$$-A \pm B_N$$
$$-A_N^i \quad \pm B_N^i$$

(f)

$$+A \pm B_N$$
$$|$$
$$+A_N^i$$
$$|$$
$$\pm B_N^i$$

(g)

$$\Box A_N^i$$
$$|$$
$$A_K^i$$

(h)

$$\Diamond A_N^i$$
$$|$$
$$A_K^i$$

(i)

$$-A \pm B_f$$
$$-A_f^i \quad \pm B_f^i$$

(j)

$$+A \pm B_f$$
$$|$$
$$+A_f^i$$
$$|$$
$$\pm B_{f'}^i$$

(k)

Diagram 1: Expansion rules for a family of term logics. (a)-(b) Rules for TFL^α. (c)-(e) Rules for TFL^ν. (f)-(i) Rules for TFL^μ. (j)-(g) Rules for TFL^ρ.

Diagrams 1a and 1b depict the rules for TFL^α. After applying a rule we introduce some index $i \in \{1, 2, 3, \ldots\}$. For statements whose initial term has a minus, "$-$" (i.e. universal statements) the index may be any natural; for statements whose initial term has a plus, "$+$" (i.e. particular statements) the index has to be a new natural if they do not already have an index. Also, following TFL tenets, we assume the next rules of rejection: $-(\pm A) = \mp A$, $-(\pm A \pm B) = \mp A \mp B$, and $-(--A--A) = +(-A) + (-A)$.

Diagrams 1c, 1d, and 1e depict the rules for TFL^ν. They work exactly as the rules for TFL^α, but notice that after applying a rule we create a vector v by keeping track of the numerical value n. Finally, Diagram 1e is a rule for ordering atomic terms with a "$+$" attached. Also notice, we need to make a little syntax modification that will come in handy in due time: we add the

14

predicate term of a statement an arbitrary number $\varepsilon > \mathsf{n}$ for any other $\mathsf{n} \in \Re^+$.

Diagrams 1f-1i depict the rules for TFL^μ. In particular, in Diagrams 1f-1g, after applying a rule we introduce a superindex $i \in \{1, 2, 3, \ldots\}$ and we let the subindex fixed as is. For statements whose initial term has a minus, the superindex may be any number; for statements whose initial term has a plus, the superindex needs to be a new number if they do not already have an index. And in particular, in Diagrams 1h-1i, after applying a rule we introduce a subindex $K \in \{1, 2, 3, \ldots\}$ and we let the superindex fixed as is. For statements whose initial operator is $\square$, the subindex may be any number; for statements whose initial term is $\diamond$, the subindex has to be a new number if they do not already have an index.

For these logics—i.e. TFL^α, TFL^ν, and TFL^μ—, a tableau is *complete* if and only if every rule that can be applied has been applied. For TFL^α, a branch is *closed* if and only if there are terms of the form $\pm A^i$ and $\mp A^i$ on two of its nodes (or $\pm_n A^i$ and $\mp_n A^i$ for TFL^ν; or $\pm A_N^i$ and $\mp A_N^i$ for TFL^μ); otherwise it is *open*. A closed branch is indicated by writing a $\perp$ at the end of it; an open branch is indicated by writing ∞. A tableau is *closed* if and only if every branch is closed; otherwise it is *open*. So, as usual, T is a logical consequence of the set of terms Γ (i.e. $\Gamma \vdash \mathsf{T}$) if and only if there is a complete closed tableau whose initial list includes the terms of Γ and the rejection of T (i.e. $\Gamma \cup \{-\mathsf{T}\} \vdash \perp$). In the case of TFL^ν we also require the vector v be equal to 0.

And finally, the rules for TFL^ρ behave as the tableaux rules for TFL^α, but besides the indexes, we introduce and keep a flag $f, f' \in \{p_i, c\}$ (p_i for premise for $i \in \{1, 2, 3, \ldots\}$, c for conclusion). For this particular logic we say a branch is *open* if and only if there are no terms of the form $\pm A^i$ and $\mp A^i$ on it; a branch is *semi-open* (or *semi-closed*) if and only if there are terms of the form $\pm A_f^i$ and $\mp A_f^i$; otherwise it is *closed*. An open branch is indicated by writing ∞ at the end of it; a semi-open (semi-closed) branch is indicated by writing $\propto_{f,f}$ ($\infty_{f,f}$); and a closed branch, as usual, is denoted by $\perp_{f,f'}$. We will return to these considerations later.

3   Mixing term logics

Meanwhile, as we can see up to this point, these different logics try to capture different aspects of natural language reasoning, namely, assertion (TFL^α), numeracy (TFL^ν), modality (TFL^μ) and causal relevance (TFL^ρ), using a term syntax; plus, it is also easy to see that, given the languages and deductive bases of each logic, we can mix—splice and split—these logics by addition and substraction of syntactical elements and rules: consider Figure 1.

Notice, thus, that $\mathsf{TFL}^{\alpha\nu} = \mathsf{TFL}^\nu$, $\mathsf{TFL}^{\alpha\mu} = \mathsf{TFL}^\mu$, and $\mathsf{TFL}^{\alpha\rho} = \mathsf{TFL}^\rho$. Then, observe that $\mathsf{TFL}^{\alpha\nu\mu} = \mathsf{TFL}^{\nu\mu}$, $\mathsf{TFL}^{\alpha\nu\rho} = \mathsf{TFL}^{\nu\rho}$, $\mathsf{TFL}^{\alpha\mu\rho} = \mathsf{TFL}^{\mu\rho}$. And finally, consider $\mathsf{TFL}^{\alpha\nu\mu\rho}$ which, in the interest of time, will be the synthetic system we will focus on.

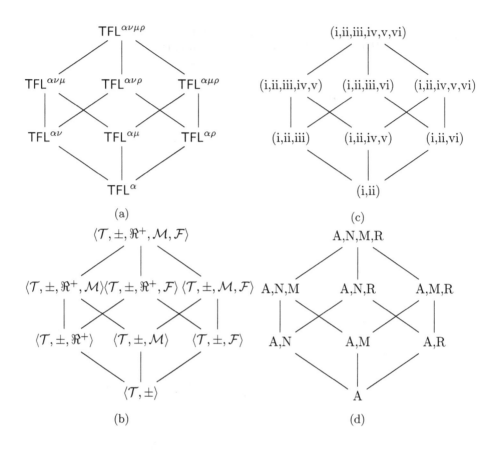

Fig. 1. (a) A family of term logics. (b) A family of languages. (c) A family of rules. (d) A family of natural language reasoning aspects (A for *assertion*, N for *numeracy*, M for *modality*, and R for *relevance*).

Thus, given the language $\mathcal{L}_{\mathsf{TFL}^{\alpha\nu\mu\rho}} = \langle \mathcal{T}, \pm, \Re^+, \mathcal{M}, \mathcal{F} \rangle$, we say:

Definition 3.1 [Synthetic statement in $\mathsf{TFL}^{\alpha\nu\mu\rho}$] A synthetic statement in $\mathsf{TFL}^{\alpha\nu\mu\rho}$ is a statement of the form:

$$\mu(\pm_n\mathsf{S} \pm_\varepsilon \mathsf{P})_f \,|\, \pm_n\mathsf{S} \pm_\varepsilon \mathsf{P}_f \,|\, \pm_n\mathsf{S} \pm \mu_\varepsilon \mathsf{P}_f$$

where μ are modalities, $\pm$ are functors, $n, \varepsilon \in \Re^+$, f is a flag, and S and P are term-schemes.

And hence, following our exposition pattern we also say:

Definition 3.2 [Valid syllogism (in $\mathsf{TFL}^{\alpha\nu\mu\rho}$)] A syllogism is valid (in $\mathsf{TFL}^{\alpha\nu\mu\rho}$) iff:

(i) The algebraic sum of the premises is equal to the conclusion,

(ii) the number of particular conclusions (*viz.*, zero or one) is equal to the number of particular premises,

(iii) either *(a)* the value of a universal conclusion is equal to the sum of the values of the universal premises, or *(b)* the value of a particular conclusion is equal to the difference of the universal premise minus the particular,

(iv) the conclusion is not stronger than any premise,

(v) the number of *de dicto*-◇ premises is not greater than the number of *de dicto*-◇ conclusions, and

(vi) all the flags of the premises are reclaimed for reaching the conclusion while the flags of the conclusion are different to the flags of the premises.

Consequently, for example, we can express the following syllogism in $\mathsf{TFL}^{\alpha\nu\mu\rho}$, call it a synthethic syllogism:

	Statement	$\mathsf{TFL}^{\alpha\nu\mu\rho}$
1.	Necessarily all philosophers are smart.	$\Box(-_0P +_\varepsilon S)_{p_1}$
2.	More than 5 logicians are possibly philosophers.	$+5L +_\varepsilon \Diamond P_{p_2}$
⊢	Possibly at least 5 logicians are possibly smart.	$\Diamond(+_5L +_\varepsilon \Diamond S)_c$

Table 10

A valid synthetic inference.

Clearly, the example shown in Table 10 is valid because (i) the algebraic sum of the premises is equal to the conclusion, and (ii) the number of particular conclusions is equal to the number of particular premises (i.e. $(-P + S) + (+L + P) = +S + L$); (iiib) the value of the particular conclusion is equal to the difference of the universal premise minus the particular (i.e. -0+5=+5); (iv) the conclusion is not stronger than any premise (i.e. from the *de dicto* standpoint, the conclusion is weaker than any premise; and the same happens from a *de re* perspective, for the terms in the conclusion are weaker than the terms in the premises); (v) the number of *de dicto*-◇ premises is not greater than the number of *de dicto*-◇ conclusions (i.e. we have 0 *de dicto* premises); and all the flags of the premises are reclaimed for reaching the conclusion while the flags of the conclusion are different to the flags of the premises.

But since these term logics are not restricted to syllogism-like inferences, we can consider multipremissed inferences (i.e. inferences with more than 2 premises) that encompasses assertion (plus relations), numeracy (both exceptive and non-exceptive), modality (both *de dicto* and *de re*) and causal relevance (Table 5).

17

	Statement	TFL$^{\alpha\nu\mu\rho}$
1.	Necessarily all but 2 A give 4 B to some C.	$\Box(-_2A + (+_\varepsilon G +_4 B +_\varepsilon C))_{p_1}$
2.	At least 5 D are necessarily A.	$+_5D +_\varepsilon \Box A_{p_2}$
3.	Every B is E.	$-_0B +_\varepsilon E_{p_3}$
⊢	Possibly 3 D give 4 E to some possible C.	$\Diamond(+_3D + (+_\varepsilon G +_4 E +_\varepsilon \Diamond C))_c$

Table 11

Another synthetic syllogism.

From these examples we can learn that we can represent different aspects of natural language reasoning. The invariable speech act of assertion—either affirmation or negation—is captured by the very use of terms and functors; numeracy is represented by the use of n (notice that when $\mathsf{n} = 0$ or $\mathsf{n} = 1$, TFL^ν collapses with TFL^α); the different ways or modes of assertion are captured by the use of modalities (notice that when the modalities are absent, TFL^μ collapses with TFL^α); and relevance is captured by the use of premise or conclusion flags.

Further, since we need to expand the aforementioned notion of validity beyond syllogistic structures, we can mix—split and splice—the previous tableaux rules as in Diagram 2. Thus, as expected, for this synthetic system we say a branch is *open* if and only if there are no terms of the form $\pm A^i_{Nf}$ and $\mp A^i_{Nf}$ on it; a branch is *semi-open* (or *semi-closed*) if and only if there are terms of the form $\pm A^i_{Nf}$ and $\mp A^i_{Nf}$; otherwise it is *closed*. An open branch is indicated by writing ∞ at the end of it; a semi-open (semi-closed) branch is indicated by writing $\propto_{f,f}$ ($\infty_{f,f}$); and a closed branch, as usual, is denoted by $\bot_{f,f'}$.

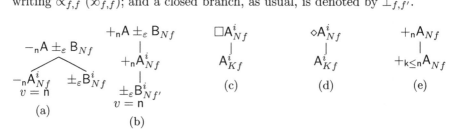

Diagram 2: TFL$^{\alpha\nu\mu\rho}$ expansion rules

Consider, as an example, the tableau for the inference shown in Table 11: Diagram 3. Lines 1 to 3 are the premises. Line 4 is the rejection of the conclusion. Line 5 is an equivalence from line 4. Lines 6 and 7 result from applying the rule in Diagram 2b to line 2, so we start $v = 5$, we introduce superindex 1, keep subindex 0, and occupy the corresponding flags. Line 8 results from applying the rule in Diagram 2e to line 6. Line 9 is the result of applying the rule in Diagram 2c to line 7, keeping the same indexes and flag, since we want the indexes to unify; similarly, line 10 is the result of applying the rule in Diagram 2c to line 9: we use number 2 since we want the numbers to unify. Line 11 results from using rule in Diagram 2c to line 1. Line 12 is the result of applying the rule in Diagram 1a to 11, so we add -2 to v; also, notice the left branch in line 12 has to be closed given the node in line 10; the right branch, however, is still open, and so we apply the rule in Diagram 2b to that open branch, getting lines 13-15, and so we add $+4$ to v. Line 16 is the application of the rule in Diagram 2e to line 14. Line 17 is the application of the rule in Diagram 2c to line 5; line 18 is just an equivalence of 17. Line 19 is the result of applying the rule in Diagram 2a to 18: notice that we have to add -3 to v, and that the left branch in 19 gets closed given the node in line 8; while the right branch in 19 still open, and so we apply an equivalence in 20. Line 21 results from applying the rule in Diagram 2a to line 20: the left branch closes given the node in line 13, but since the right branch in 21 is still open, we apply an equivalence in 22. Line 23 results from using the rule in Diagram 2a to line 22. Line 23 results from using the rule in Diagram 2a to line 3: observe the left branch has to be closed given the node in line 16; but since the right branch is still open, we use the rule in Diagram 2e on it as to obtain line 24. Line 25 results from applying the rule in Diagram 2a to line 22: the left branch closes given the node in line 24 and we add -4 to v, but the left branch is still open. We use an equivalence in 26, and then we use the rule in Diagram 2c to 26 in order to obtain 27, and so this last branch is closed given the node in line 15. Hence, since the tableau is closed, complete, $v = 0$, and all the flags are different and carried at the end of every tip, we say this synthetic syllogism is valid.

4   Final remarks

Natural language reasoning is a complex inferential procedure that may include, beyond the speech act of assertion, information about numeracy, modality, and causal relevance. Given this premise, we have combined four term logics that try to capture each one of those aspects and then we have extended the notions of validity of said logics by mixing their respective tableaux. Finally, to wrap this up, let us briefly consider some potential objections and comments regarding future work.

Objection 1. This is unnecesary. While it is true that this proposal can be deemed unnecessary, one problem with this objection is that, put like this, it seems very deflationary: one could ask what is the utility of any scientific endeavour. But this, then, would not be an objection to the proposal, but to almost any human activity. Of course, someone might still say that this answer is rather weak, for we require a more specific response. So, consider that we can pinpoint, at least, a couple of specific purposes: *i)* the study and development of systems like these contribute to the research of natural language reasoning using formal tools beyond the usual Fregean first order logics; and *ii)* these systems can be further developed as to promote the use of non-classical programming paradigms for logic programming as in [8].

Objection 2. This is too complex. It is also true that, at first glance, the proposal seems too complex of a contraption; now, that is a good observation, but is not a very good objection. For one, it would be quite counterintuitive to

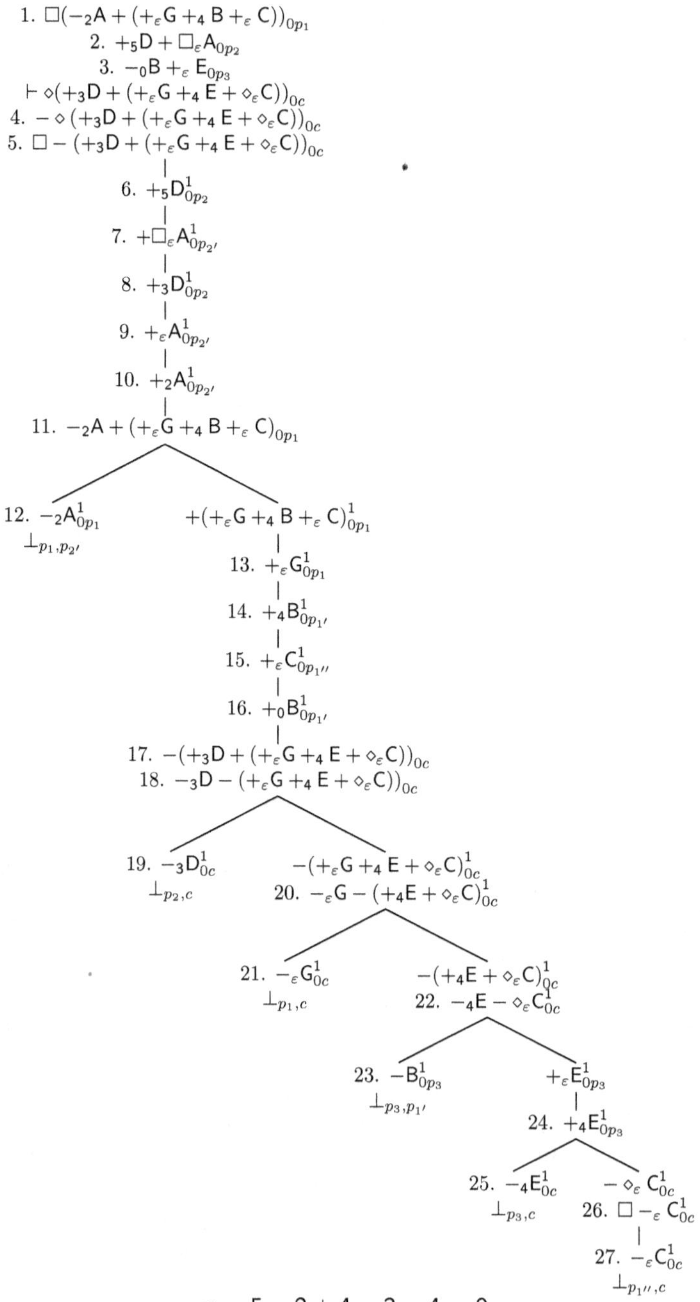

1. $\square(-_2A + (+_\varepsilon G +_4 B +_\varepsilon C))_{0p_1}$
2. $+_5D + \square_\varepsilon A_{0p_2}$
3. $-_0B +_\varepsilon E_{0p_3}$
$\vdash \diamond(+_3D + (+_\varepsilon G +_4 E + \diamond_\varepsilon C))_{0c}$
4. $- \diamond (+_3D + (+_\varepsilon G +_4 E + \diamond_\varepsilon C))_{0c}$
5. $\square - (+_3D + (+_\varepsilon G +_4 E + \diamond_\varepsilon C))_{0c}$

6. $+_5D^1_{0p_2}$

7. $+\square_\varepsilon A^1_{0p_{2'}}$

8. $+_3D^1_{0p_2}$

9. $+_\varepsilon A^1_{0p_{2'}}$

10. $+_2A^1_{0p_{2'}}$

11. $-_2A + (+_\varepsilon G +_4 B +_\varepsilon C)_{0p_1}$

12. $-_2A^1_{0p_1}$ $+(+_\varepsilon G +_4 B +_\varepsilon C)^1_{0p_1}$
$\perp_{p_1, p_{2'}}$

13. $+_\varepsilon G^1_{0p_1}$

14. $+_4B^1_{0p_{1'}}$

15. $+_\varepsilon C^1_{0p_{1''}}$

16. $+_0B^1_{0p_{1'}}$

17. $-(+_3D + (+_\varepsilon G +_4 E + \diamond_\varepsilon C))_{0c}$
18. $-_3D - (+_\varepsilon G +_4 E + \diamond_\varepsilon C)_{0c}$

19. $-_3D^1_{0c}$ $-(+_\varepsilon G +_4 E + \diamond_\varepsilon C)^1_{0c}$
$\perp_{p_2, c}$ 20. $-_\varepsilon G - (+_4E + \diamond_\varepsilon C)^1_{0c}$

21. $-_\varepsilon G^1_{0c}$ $-(+_4E + \diamond_\varepsilon C)^1_{0c}$
$\perp_{p_1, c}$ 22. $-_4E - \diamond_\varepsilon C^1_{0c}$

23. $-B^1_{0p_3}$ $+_\varepsilon E^1_{0p_3}$
$\perp_{p_3, p_{1'}}$ 24. $+_4E^1_{0p_3}$

25. $-_4E^1_{0c}$ $- \diamond_\varepsilon C^1_{0c}$
$\perp_{p_3, c}$ 26. $\square -_\varepsilon C^1_{0c}$

27. $-_\varepsilon C^1_{0c}$
$\perp_{p_{1''}, c}$

$$v = 5 - 2 + 4 - 3 - 4 = 0$$

Diagram 3: A valid synthetic syllogism.

say that we do not need to study or develop higher order logics, hybrid logics, or non-classical logics because they are more complex and make logical analysis even harder. The problem with this objection is that it fails to recognize the net gain of complex models. Thus, even if combining these term logics seems to increase complexity, that is not a price to high to pay if we consider the net benefits of synthetizing four different aspects of natural language reasoning. As a reviewer has correctly pointed out: a proposal like this could provides a good trade-off between expressive power and tractability.

Objection 3. This is too ambiguous. And finally, while it is true that the concept of mixing for term logics is still ambiguous, it seems the failure to communicate comes from our exposition: we have not enough space to develop the whole formal theory behind the combination of term logics, but that does not imply the very proposal is ambiguous in itself: in other place we have offered more insights on this issue, but for the purposes of this contribution, it suffices to say that mixing term logics amounts to mixing a rules and signatures.

Finally, given these challenges, we would like to mention some of our future work: *i)* we need to explain the formal theory behind the combination of term logics, including proofs of completeness; *ii)* we also need to compare the net benefits of this synthetic logic *vis-à-vis* Fregean logics; and finally, *iii)* we require more time to offer minutiae about implementation.

Acknowledgements

We would like to thank the anonymous reviewers for the precise corrections and useful suggestions. This research was funded by an UPAEP Research Grant.

References

[1] Becker, A., "Die Aristotelische Theorie der Möglichkeitsschlüsse," Wissenschaftliche Buchgesellschaft, 1968.

[2] Bocheński, J., "Formale Logik," Orbis academicus ; ; 3, Karl Alber, 1962.

[3] Carnap, R., *Die alte und die neue logik*, Erkenntnis **1** (1930), pp. 12–26.
URL http://www.jstor.org/stable/20011586

[4] Castro-Manzano, J.-M., *Silogística intermedia, términos y árboles*, Tópicos, Revista De Filosofía (2019), pp. 209–237.

[5] Castro-Manzano, J.-M., *Distribution tableaux, distribution models*, Axioms **9** (2020).
URL https://www.mdpi.com/2075-1680/9/2/41

[6] Castro-Manzano, J. M., *Murphree's numerical term logic tableaux*, Electronic Notes in Theoretical Computer Science **354** (2020), pp. 17–28, proceedings of the Eleventh and Twelfth Latin American Workshop on Logic/Languages, Algorithms and New Methods of Reasoning (LANMR).
URL https://www.sciencedirect.com/science/article/pii/S1571066120300797

[7] Castro-Manzano, J.-M., *Un método de árboles para la silogística modal*, Open Insight, Revista De Filosofía (2020), pp. 209–237.

[8] Castro-Manzano, J.-M., *Traditional logic and computational thinking*, Philosophies **6** (2021).
URL https://www.mdpi.com/2409-9287/6/1/12

[9] Castro-Manzano, J.-M. and P.-O. Reyes-Cardenas, *Term functor logic tableaux*, South American Journal of Logic **4** (2018), pp. 9–50.

[10] D'Agostino, M., D. M. Gabbay, R. Hähnle and J. Posegga, "Handbook of Tableau Methods," Springer, 1999.

[11] de Morgan, A., *On the Syllogism, No. IV., and on the Logic of Relations*, Transactions of the Cambridge Philosophical Society **10** (1864), p. 331.

[12] Englebretsen, G., "The New Syllogistic," 05, P. Lang, 1987.

[13] Englebretsen, G., *Preliminary notes on a new modal syllogistic.*, Notre Dame J. Formal Logic **29** (1988), pp. 381–395.
URL https://doi.org/10.1305/ndjfl/1093637935

[14] Englebretsen, G., "Something to Reckon with: The Logic of Terms," Canadian electronic library: Books collection, University of Ottawa Press, 1996.

[15] Englebretsen, G., "Robust Reality: An Essay in Formal Ontology," Philosophische Analyse / Philosophical Analysis, De Gruyter, 2013.

[16] Englebretsen, G., "Bare Facts and Naked Truths: A New Correspondence Theory of Truth," Taylor & Francis, 2017.

[17] Englebretsen, G. and C. Sayward, "Philosophical Logic: An Introduction to Advanced Topics," Bloomsbury Academic, 2011.

[18] Frege, G. and I. Angelelli, "Begriffsschrift und andere Aufsätze," Wissenschaftliche Buchgesellschaft, 1973.

[19] Geach, P. T., "Reference and Generality: An Examination of Some Medieval and Modern Theories," Contemporary Philosophy / Cornell University, Cornell University Press, 1962.

[20] Haack, S., "Philosophy of Logics," Cambridge University Press, 1978.

[21] Hintikka, J. and K. Hintikka, "Time & Necessity: Studies in Aristotle's Theory of Modality," Clarendon Press, 1973.

[22] Kneale, W., M. William Kneale, W. Kneale, M. Kneale, A. Conte and O. U. Press, "The Development of Logic," Clarendon Press, 1962.

[23] Kreeft, P. and T. Dougherty, "Socratic Logic: A Logic Text Using Socratic Method, Platonic Questions & Aristotelian Principles," St. Augustine's Press, 2004.

[24] Kuhn, S. T., *An axiomatization of predicate functor logic.*, Notre Dame J. Formal Logic **24** (1983), pp. 233–241.
URL https://doi.org/10.1305/ndjfl/1093870313

[25] Łukasiewicz, J., "Aristotle's syllogistic from the standpoint of modern formal logic," Clarendon Press, 1957.

[26] Malink, M., "Aristotle's Modal Syllogistic," Harvard University Press, 2013.
URL https://books.google.com.mx/books?id=qQ90AQAAQBAJ

[27] McCall, S., "Aristotle's Modal Syllogisms," Studies in logic and the foundations of mathematics, North-Holland Publishing Company, 1963.

[28] Moss, L., *Natural logic*, in: S. Lappin and C. Fox, editors, *The Handbook of Contemporary Semantic Theory*, John Wiley & Sons, 2015 .

[29] Murphree, W. A., *Numerical term logic*, Notre Dame J. Formal Logic **39** (1998), pp. 346–362.
URL https://doi.org/10.1305/ndjfl/1039182251

[30] Noah, A., *Predicate-functors and the limits of decidability in logic.*, Notre Dame J. Formal Logic **21** (1980), pp. 701–707.
URL https://doi.org/10.1305/ndjfl/1093883255

[31] Priest, G., "An Introduction to Non-Classical Logic: From If to Is," Cambridge Introductions to Philosophy, Cambridge University Press, 2008.

[32] Quine, W. V. O., *Predicate functor logic*, in: J. E. Fenstad, editor, *Proceedings of the Second Scandinavian Logic Symposium* (1971).

[33] Rini, A. A., *Is there a modal syllogistic?*, Notre Dame J. Formal Logic **39** (1998), pp. 554–572.
URL https://doi.org/10.1305/ndjfl/1039118870

[34] Russell, B., "A Critical Exposition of the Philosophy of Leibniz: With an Appendix of Leading Passages," Cambridge University Press.

[35] Sommers, F., *On a fregean dogma*, in: I. Lakatos, editor, *Problems in the Philosophy of Mathematics*, Studies in Logic and the Foundations of Mathematics **47**, Elsevier, 1967 pp. 47 – 81.
URL http://www.sciencedirect.com/science/article/pii/S0049237X08715210

[36] Sommers, F., "The Logic of Natural Language," Clarendon Library of Logic and Philosophy, Clarendon Press; Oxford: New York: Oxford University Press, 1982.

[37] Sommers, F., *Intelectual autobiography*, in: D. S. Oderberg, editor, *The Old New Logic: Essays on the Philosophy of Fred Sommers*, Bradford book, 2005 pp. 1 – 24.

[38] Sommers, F. and G. Englebretsen, "An Invitation to Formal Reasoning: The Logic of Terms," Ashgate, 2000.

[39] Striker, G., *Assertoric vs modal syllogistic*, Ancient Philosophy **14** (1994), pp. 39–51.

[40] Szabolcsi, L. and G. Englebretsen, "Numerical Term Logic," Edwin Mellen Press, 2008.

[41] Thom, P., "Logic and Ontology in the Syllogistic of Robert Kilwardby," Studien Und Texte Zur Geistesgeschichte Des Mittelalters, Brill, 2007.

[42] Thom, P., "The Logic of Essentialism: An Interpretation of Aristotles Modal Syllogistic," The New Synthese Historical Library, Springer Netherlands, 2012.

[43] Thompson, B., *Syllogisms using "few", "many", and "most".*, Notre Dame J. Formal Logic **23** (1982), pp. 75–84.
URL https://doi.org/10.1305/ndjfl/1093883568

[44] Thompson, B., *Syllogisms with statistical quantifiers.*, Notre Dame J. Formal Logic **27** (1986), pp. 93–103.
URL https://doi.org/10.1305/ndjfl/1093636527

[45] Woods, J., "Aristotle's Earlier Logic," Studies in Logic, College Publications, 2014.

[46] Woods, J., "Logic Naturalized," Springer International Publishing, Cham, 2016 pp. 403–432.

Calculi and Models for Non-Horn Knowledge Bases Containing Neural and Evaluable Predicates

Alexander Sakharov

Synstretch
Framingham, Massachusetts, USA

Abstract

This paper investigates logical foundations of the derivation of literals from non-Horn knowledge bases with fuzzy predicates. Some of the predicates are defined by neural networks, and some are defined by recursive functions. This inference excludes reasoning by contradiction, and it is characterized by means of substructural single-succedent sequent calculi with non-logical axioms expressing knowledge base rules and facts. The semantics of this inference is specified by constrained real-valued models. Lower bounds of fuzzy truth values of ground literals are calculated by traversing sequent calculus derivations of the literals.

Keywords: non-Horn rule, sequent calculus, fuzzy knowledge base, real-valued logic, neural-symbolic computing

1 Introduction

The languages of logic programs and knowledge bases (KB) are usually based on first-order logic (FOL) [29]. Most commonly, KB facts are atoms or literals. Atoms are expressions $P(t_1, ..., t_k)$ where P is a predicate and $t_1, ..., t_k$ are terms. Literals are atoms or their negations. Non-Horn rules are expressions $A \Leftarrow A_1 \wedge ... \wedge A_k$, where $A, A_1, ..., A_k$ are literals. In Horn rules, A and all A_i are atoms. In normal logic programs, A is an atom and A_i are literals.

Horn KBs have a limited inference power. The advantages of non-Horn KB over normal logic programs are discussed in [31]. The semantics of non-Horn KBs is given by classical 2-valued FOL models. FOL calculi are used as the proof theories of non-Horn KBs. Nonetheless, inference for KBs and logic programs differs significantly from inference in FOL. Most importantly, the outcome of this inference and its intermediate steps is literal sets as opposed to arbitrary FOL formulas.

KBs and logic programs may include computable (aka evaluable) functions and predicates [21]. The values of terms composed of constants and evaluable functions are calculated during inference. Also, the truth values of atoms of evaluable predicates with constant arguments are calculated, not derived.

Evaluable functions and predicates may be partial. Evaluable predicates do not have to be boolean, they may yield multiple truth values.

Recent advances in AI made it possible to implement some predicates as neural networks [9,33,15,32,13]. Representing predicates by neural networks is also known as relational embedding. These predicates are usually represented by tensor expressions whose coefficients are learned. The fuzzy truth values of atoms of these neural predicates with constant arguments are calculated by substituting argument embeddings into the tensor expressions. These truth values are real numbers. Integration of neural methods with symbolic reasoning is a challenging problem and an area of intense research [7,19]. For some predicates, the calculation of fuzzy truth values of atoms with constant arguments can be implemented by other means than neural networks.

The principle of Reductio Ad Absurdum (RAA) states that if A is deduced from a hypothesis that is A's complement, then A is derivable. Reasoning by contradiction, i.e. with using RAA, is not quite adequate for KBs with evaluable predicates [30]. It will be explained later that reasoning by contradiction is not appropriate for KBs with neural predicates either.

The aim of this paper is to specify model and proof theories for inference from KBs containing neural and evaluable predicates along with other predicates that are derivable from KB rules and facts. In section 3, KB inference without RAA is characterized by sequent calculi with a limited set of logical and structural rules and with non-logical axioms that are images of KB facts and rules. In section 4, the semantics of inference from KBs containing neural and evaluable predicates is specified by constrained real-valued models. It is also shown how to calculate lower bounds of the truth values of derived ground literals.

2   Non-Horn Knowledge Bases With Fuzzy Predicates

Let us recall some definitions which will be used later. A KB is called consistent if no atom is a fact or is derivable from this KB, along with its negation being derivable or a fact. A literal is called ground if it does not contain variables. A substitution is a finite set of mappings of variables to terms. The result of applying a substitution to a formula or set of formulas is called its instance.

We consider inference of ground literals, which are called goals, from non-Horn KBs. These KBs may contain predicates specified by neural networks, which are used to approximate the truth values of atoms of these predicates with constant arguments. Fuzzy truth values are usually represented by real numbers from interval $[0, 1]$. For non-Horn KBs, it is more convenient to use interval $[-1, 1]$ for the representation of truth values. One represents true, minus one represents false. Other real numbers from interval $[-1, 1]$ represent fuzzy truth values. Neural methods and their implementation are not discussed here because our approach is applicable to a variety of neural networks. The only requirement to these networks is that they yield numbers from interval $[-1, 1]$ for any input data.

These KBs may also contain evaluable functions and predicates [21].

We assume that evaluable functions and predicates are defined as recursive functions in a functional programming language or as algorithms in a procedural programming language. The truth values yielded by the algorithms implementing evaluable predicates could also be fuzzy, i.e. they could be from interval $[-1, 1]$.

Terms of evaluable functions with constant arguments are evaluated as soon as they appear in KB derivations. The same applies to atoms of neural and evaluable predicates with constant arguments. The evaluation may not terminate, in which case it is assumed that the truth value is zero. Any complete search strategy for inference from KBs with evaluable and neural predicates should continue and-or search [29] simultaneously with the evaluations including neural computations. If the evaluation of ground atom $A(...)$ yields a positive value above a certain threshold $h > 0$, then $A(...)$ is considered a KB fact. If the evaluation of this atom yields a negative value below $-h$, then $\neg A(...)$ is considered a fact. Non-Horn rules are well-suited for KBs with neural and evaluable predicates because these negative facts correspond to literals in KB rules.

All other predicates will be called derivable. As explained in [31], derivable predicates should be considered partial by default. In the presence of neural predicates, the truth values of ground atoms of derivable predicates should also be real numbers from interval $[-1, 1]$, that is, derivable predicates like neural ones are fuzzy. It is expected that fuzzy truth values higher than h are assigned to some facts. One is the default truth value for KB facts. Let $|A|$ denote the truth value of formula A.

We rely on the traditional definition of truth functions in fuzzy KBs [4]. The following equation defines the truth values for negation: $|\neg A| = -|A|$. The use of this truth function for negation is limited to the calculation of the truth values of negatibve literals. The truth values for conjunction are defined by the following equation: $|A_1 \wedge ... \wedge A_k| = \min\{|A_1|, ..., |A_k|\}$. This function is called the Godel t-norm. The use of this truth function for conjuction is limited to the calculation of the truth values of the bodies of KB rules.

Truth functions for disjunctions will not be used here, and the use of implication truth functions will be indirect in the KBs under consideration. The meaning of KB rules is that the truth value of the rule body is a lower bound of the truth value of the head. Given that KB rules are implications and assuming that KB rules are not fuzzy, this semantics of KB rules is consistent with residuum functions for t-norms. For the residua of the Lukasiewicz, Godel, and product t-norms, $|A \Rightarrow B| = 1$ if and only if $|A| \leq |B|$ [12].

It is explained in [31] why reasoning by contradiction is questionable for KBs with evaluable predicates. The same argument applies to KBs containing neural predicates. Consider two KB rules $P \Leftarrow Q$ and $P \Leftarrow \neg Q$. Here is reasoning by contradiction using these rules. Suppose P is false. The first rule implies that Q is false, and hence P is true by the second rule. Now suppose $|P| = 0$. If $|Q| = 0$ as well, then both rules are satisfied, but they do not provide any evidence that P is true or $|P| > 0$ at least.

3   Sequent Calculi

Let $-A$ denote the complement of A, i.e. it is the negation of atom A, and the atom of negative literal A. A sequent is $\Gamma \vdash \Pi$ where Γ is an antecedent and Π is a succedent. Antecedents and succedents are multisets of formulas. KB inference and logic programming are concerned about the derivation of literals, i.e. sequents of the form $\vdash A$ where A is a literal. Consider single-succedent calculi in which formulas are literals. The only structural rule is *cut*.

$$\frac{\Gamma \vdash A \quad A, \Pi \vdash B}{\Gamma, \Pi \vdash B} \; cut$$

These sequent calculi do not have logical axioms. The following rule is the only logical rule. It replaces the standard negation rules.

$$\frac{A, \Gamma \vdash B}{-B, \Gamma \vdash -A} \; swap$$

KB facts and rules can be treated as non-logical axioms [23]. Sequents of the form $\vdash A$ represent facts, and rules are represented by sequents of the form $A_1, ..., A_n \vdash A$ where $A, A_1, ..., A_n$ are literals. Variables can be replaced by any terms in instances of these axioms.

Definition 3.1 L_{cs} is the set of single-succedent sequent calculus instances in which formulas are literals, succedents contain one literal, the structural rule is *cut*, the logical rule is *swap*, and non-logical axioms represent KB rules and facts.

Arguably, L_{cs} are some of the simplest calculi formalizing KB inference without RAA. Alternatively, this inference could be formalized by calculi whose sequents contain atoms only. Yet another option is to define calculi based on clauses, i.e. disjunctions, as opposed to sequents. We chose L_{cs} because their single-succedent sequents comprised of literals copy KB rules. The other two options require KB rule transformations. L_{cs} rules embody two fundamental logical principles: *cut* corresponds to Modus Ponens and *swap* corresponds to Modus Tollens.

Usually, if a formal theory is inconsistent, then any formula is derivable in this theory. This is why inconsistent theories are discarded. In reality, KBs may have bugs and may be inconsistent. Proliferation of inconsistencies is limited in L_{cs}. Unlike sequent calculi for FOL, nothing else could be derived in L_{cs} from sequents $\vdash A$ and $\vdash \neg A$ alone. Nonproliferation of inconsistencies is important in KB development because bugs do not lead to a mass of gibberish results in this case.

Theorem 3.2 *(normal form) Any L_{cs} derivation of literal G can be transformed into such L_{cs} derivation of G that the premise of every swap is a KB rule and the transformed derivation tree contains the same KB fact instances as the original derivation tree.*

Proof. Consider a L_{cs} derivation. Let us replace *swap* with the two following rules and adjust the derivation by replacing *swap* with the $L\neg$ rule followed by the $R\neg$ rule.

$$\frac{\Gamma \vdash A}{-A, \Gamma \vdash} \; L- \qquad\qquad \frac{B, \Gamma \vdash}{\Gamma \vdash -B} \; R-$$

The $L-$ and $R-$ rules can be moved upward.

$$\frac{\dfrac{\Gamma \vdash A \quad A, \Pi \vdash B}{\Gamma, \Pi \vdash B}}{-B, \Gamma, \Pi \vdash} \qquad \rightarrow \qquad \frac{\Gamma \vdash A \quad \dfrac{A, \Pi \vdash B}{A, -B, \Pi \vdash}}{-B, \Gamma, \Pi \vdash}$$

$$\frac{\dfrac{\Gamma \vdash A \quad A, \Pi, B \vdash}{\Gamma, \Pi, B \vdash}}{\Gamma, \Pi \vdash -B} \qquad \rightarrow \qquad \frac{\Gamma \vdash A \quad \dfrac{A, \Pi, B \vdash}{A, \Pi \vdash -B}}{\Gamma, \Pi \vdash -B}$$

$$\frac{\dfrac{B, \Gamma \vdash A \quad A, \Pi \vdash}{B, \Gamma, \Pi \vdash}}{\Gamma, \Pi \vdash -B} \qquad \rightarrow \qquad \frac{\dfrac{A, \Pi \vdash}{\Pi \vdash -A} \quad \dfrac{\dfrac{B, \Gamma \vdash A}{-A, B, \Gamma \vdash}}{-A, \Gamma \vdash -B}}{\Gamma, \Pi \vdash -B}$$

By repeatedly applying these permutations, all applications of the $L-/R-$ rules can be moved above all applications of *cut*. Since $R\neg$ always follows $L\neg$, the succedents of the premises of all *cut* rules are single literals. Any sequence of $L-/R-$ rules applied to a KB rule or fact can be either discarded or replaced by one *swap* rule. The above permutations do not change the set of KB fact instances. Hence, the transformed derivation satisfies the statement of this theorem. $\square$

Theorem 3.3 L_{cs} *is sound and complete with respect to the derivation of ground literals in FOL without RAA.*

Proof. It is proved in [30] that ground literal L is derivable from KB facts and rules in FOL without RAA if and only if $-L$ is refutable by resolution in which the factoring rule is not used and at least one premise of every resolution step is not $-L$ or its descendant. Consider such resolution refutation. As usual, the resolution steps that are not ascendants of the endclause are discarded. Let us ground this refutation and then exclude the step that resolves $-L$. There is only one such step because at least one premise of every resolution step is not $-L$ or its descendant. As a result, L is added to every descendant clause of this step including the endclause which becomes L.

Let us traverse this resolution tree bottom-up and map every resolution step to an application of *cut* in L_{cs}. Sequent $\vdash L$ is the conclusion of the last *cut* in the respective L_{cs} derivation tree. The premises of every *cut* in this tree are uniquely determined by the resolution step. The succedent of the *cut* conclusion is also the succedent of the second premise, and the succedent of the first premise is the principal formula of this *cut*. Every leaf node in the L_{cs} derivation tree is an instance of a KB fact, an instance of a KB rule, or a sequent that is the conclusion of *swap* applied to an instance of a KB rule. Hence, the resulting tree is a normal-form L_{cs} derivation.

Now consider a ground normal-form L_{cs} derivation of sequent $\vdash L$. Every application of the *cut* rule in this derivation corresponds to a resolution step, and ground instances of KB rules and facts are used as input clauses in this resolution derivation instead of the rules and facts. The endclause of this resolution derivation is L.

The lifting lemma [6] states that if clause A is an instance of A', B is an instance of B', and C is the resolvent of A and B, then there is such clause C' that C is its instance, and C' is the resolvent of A' and B'. It is well-known that the lifting lemma can be generalized onto arbitrary resolution derivations: If C is the endclause of a resolution derivation with input clauses $A_1, ..., A_n$ which are instances of $A'_1, ..., A'_n$, respectively, then there is such resolution derivation with input clauses $A'_1, ..., A'_n$ and endclause C' that C is an instance of C'. This is proved by a straightforward induction on the depth of resolution derivations.

As a consequence of this generalization of the lifting lemma, there is a resolution tree with the input comprised of KB rules and facts treated as clauses and with such endclause L' that L is its instance. A step resolving L' and $-L$ is added to this derivation. The resolvent of this step is the empty clause, and $-L$ occurs in one premise of the last step only. Hence, this resolution refutation corresponds to a FOL derivation without RAA.   □

4   Constrained Real-Valued Models

Models are usually defined by truth tables (or functions) for logical connectives so that the truth values of ground formulas can be calculated. No other formulas than literals are produced during KB derivations. Because of this, legitimate models for KB inference can be defined by a negation truth function and by constraints on truth values in ground instances of facts and rules as opposed to truth tables for other logical connectives.

Definition 4.1 An assignment of real numbers from interval $[-1, 1]$ to ground literals is a $\mathcal{M}_r$ model if $|\neg A| = -|A|$ for any ground atom A and the following constraints are satisfied:
1. A is a ground KB fact instance: $|A| > h$
2. $A_0 \Leftarrow A_1 \wedge ... \wedge A_k$ is a ground KB rule instance:
   a. If $|A_i| \geq h$ for $i = 1...k$, then $|A_0| \geq \min\{|A_1|, ..., |A_k|\}$.
   b. For $j = 1, ..., k$, if $|A_0| \leq -h$ and $|A_i| \geq h$ for $i = 1...j-1$ and $i = j+1...k$, then $-|A_j| \geq -|A_0|$.

Constraint 2a expresses the semantics of KB rules: the truth value of the body is less or equal to the truth value of the head, min is employed as the truth function for conjunctions of literals in the bodies. Constraint 2b is a consequence of this semantics of KB rules with fuzzy literals. Consider the case that $|A_i|$ are positive for $i = 1...j-1$ and $i = j+1...k$, and $|A_0|$ is negative. In this case, inequality $|A_0| \geq \min\{|A_1|, ..., |A_k|\}$ implies that $-|A_j| \geq -|A_0|$.

Literal A is valid regarding $\mathcal{M}_r$ models if $|A'| > h$ for all groundings A' of literal A in all $\mathcal{M}_r$ models. The constraints of $\mathcal{M}_r$ models can also be considered in the context of sequents as opposed to KB facts and rules. These constraints hold for non-logical axioms of L_{cs}.

Definition 4.2 The set of obscure occurrences of literals in derivation τ is defined recursively as the minimal set of literal occurrences satisfying the following two conditions.
- If sequent $-A_0, A_1, ..., A_{j-1}, A_{j+1}, ..., A_k \vdash -A_j$ from τ is the conclusion of *swap* applied to KB rule instance $A_0 \Leftarrow A_1 \wedge ... \wedge A_k$, then $A_1, ..., A_{j-1}, A_{j+1}, ..., A_k$ are obscure in τ.
- If sequent $A_1, ..., A_k \vdash A_0$ occurs in τ and A_0 is obscure in τ, then $A_1, .., A_k$ are obscure in it.

Let $m(\tau) = \min_{A \in \mathcal{F}} |A|$ where $\mathcal{F}$ is the set of non-obscure occurrences of ground KB fact instances in derivation τ. If $\mathcal{F} = \emptyset$, then $m(\tau) = 1$.

Theorem 4.3 *(soundness) If τ is a ground L_{cs} derivation of literal G, then $|G| \geq m(\tau) \geq h$ for all $\mathcal{M}_r$ models.*

Proof. Let us transform τ to the normal form defined in Theorem 3.2. The set of literals in τ is the same as the set of literals in its normal form. We will prove by induction on the depth of normal-form derivations that $|D| \geq \min\{|A_i|, ..., |A_j|, m(\mu)\}$ for the endsequent $A_1, ..., A_k \vdash D$ of any derivation μ, where $A_i, ..., A_j$ are non-obscure literal occurrences in μ among $A_1, ..., A_k$. As a corollary, $|G| \geq m(\tau)$. Inequality $m(\tau) \geq h$ holds because $|A| \geq h$ for all ground fact instances A.

Base: The depth of derivation μ is zero. In this case, G is an instance of a KB fact, and the above inequality holds.

Induction step. Suppose the inequality under consideration is satisfied for all derivations whose depth is less or equal n. Suppose the depth of μ is $n+1$. If the endsequent $A_1, ..., A_k \vdash D$ is a KB rule instance, then this sequent does not contain KB fact instances, and inequality $|D| \geq \min\{|A_1|, ..., |A_k|, m(\mu)\}$ holds due to constraint 2a. None of $A_1, ..., A_k$ is obscure in μ. If the last rule in μ is *swap*, then its premise is a KB rule, μ does not contain KB fact instances, and inequality $|D| \geq \min\{|A_1|, m(\mu)\}$ holds due to constraint 2b. Literals $A_2, ..., A_k$ are obscure in μ.

Now let the last rule in μ be *cut*, the first premise of this *cut* be $B_1, ..., B_k \vdash C_1$, and the second premise be $C_1, ..., C_m \vdash D$. The conclusion of this *cut* is $B_1, ..., B_k, C_2, ..., C_m \vdash D$. If δ is the derivation ending in $B_1, ..., B_k \vdash C_1$, $B_b, ..., B_{b'}$ are the non-obscure literals of this antecedent in δ, ν is the derivation ending in $C_1, ..., C_m \vdash D$, $C_c, ..., C_{c'}$ are the non-obscure literals of the antecedent of the latter sequent in ν, then $|C_1| \geq \min\{|B_b|, ..., |B_{b'}|, m(\mu)\}$ and $|D| \geq \min\{|C_c|, ..., |C_{c'}|, m(\nu)\}$ by the induction assumption.

If C_1 is obscure in ν, then it is also obscure in μ. In this case, all literal occurrences from δ including $B_1, ..., B_k$ are obscure in μ. This is proved by a straightforward induction on the depth of normal-form derivations. In the case of obscure C_1, the set of non-obscure literal occurrences of μ is the same as the set of non-obscure literal occurrences of ν. Therefore, $|D| \geq \min\{|C_c|, ..., |C_{c'}|, m(\mu)\}$.

Now, consider the case that C_1 is not obscure in ν, i.e. C_c is C_1. By a straightforward induction on the depth of normal-form derivations, the succedent of the endsequent of any derivation γ is not obscure in γ. As a corollary, C_1 is not obscure in μ. The remaining literals among $C_c, ..., C_{c'}$ are not obscure in μ either. Let $C_{c''}$ follow C_c in this list of literals. By combining the inequalities for both premises, we get $|D| \geq \min\{|B_b|, ..., |B_{b'}|, m(\delta), |C_{c''}|, ..., |C_{c'}|, m(\nu)\}$. The set of non-obscure occurrences of KB fact instances of μ is the union of the respective sets of δ and ν. Hence, $|D| \geq \min\{|B_1|, ..., |B_k|, |C_{c''}|, ..., |C_{c'}|, m(\mu)\}$. □

This theorem establishes that $m(\tau)$ is a conservative approximation of the truth values of G in $\mathcal{M}_r$ models. The proof of Theorem 3.3 shows that resolution refutations without factoring can be transformed to L_{cs} derivations in a single preorder traversal of the resolution refutations. Consequently, the time complexity of this transformation is linear in the size of the refutations.

It is clear from the proof of Theorem 4.3 that the calculation of a lower bound of $|G|$ can be done in a single postorder traversal of the L_{cs} derivation tree. Detecting obscure literal occurrences is done simultaneously with the calculation of m values during this traversal. Hence, this calculation takes a linear time of the size of G's derivation in L_{cs}.

Efficient resolution methods can be used to implement inference from non-Horn KBs containing neural and evaluable predicates. The resolution refutations are transformed into L_{cs} derivations, and then lower bounds of the fuzzy truth values of the goals are calculated. The overall time complexity of these additional computations is linear in the size of the resolution refutations. Complexity issues for advanced resolution methods are discussed in [17].

Consider the following KB rule $R(x, z) \Leftarrow R(x, y) \wedge R(y, z)$ expressing transitivity of predicate R. For instance, if a KB contains facts $|R(a, b)| = 0.5$ and $|\neg R(a, c)| = 0.8$, then nothing else can be derived from these facts and the aforementioned rule by forward chaining. Our method makes it possible to derive goal $\neg R(b, c)$ and to get this estimate: $|\neg R(b, c)| \geq 0.8$.

Theorem 4.4 *(completeness)* If $|G| \geq h$ in all $\mathcal{M}_r$ models for ground literal G, then there exists a derivation of G in L_{cs}.

Proof. Suppose G is not derivable in L_{cs} from KB facts and rules. Let us look at model M in which $|B| = 1$ for every ground literal B that is derivable from KB facts and rules, $|C| = -1$ for every such ground literal C that $-C$ is derivable, and $|D| = 0$ for every other ground literal D. Such model M exists for any consistent KB, and $|G| = 0$ in M.

Constraint 1 holds for M because ground instances of facts are derivable. Suppose constraint 2a is violated for ground KB rule instance $A_0 \Leftarrow A_1 \wedge ... \wedge A_k$. In this case, $|A_i| = 1$ for $i = 1...k$, and all sequents $\vdash A_i$ are derivable in L_{cs}. Hence, A_0 is derivable from the latter by k applications of *cut* to $A_1, ..., A_k \vdash A_0$ and to every $\vdash A_i$ for $i = 1...k$. Hence, constraint 2a could not be violated for this rule instance.

If we suppose that constraint 2b is violated for ground KB rule instance $A_0 \Leftarrow A_1 \wedge ... \wedge A_k$, then all A_i for $i = 1...j-1$ and $i = j+1...k$ are derivable in L_{cs}, and $-A_0$ is also derivable. Sequent $-A_0, A_1, ..., A_{j-1}, A_{j+1}, ..., A_k \vdash -A_j$

is derived by applying *swap* to this KB rule instance. $-A_j$ is derivable by application of *cut* to this sequent and to $\vdash -A_0$ followed by $k-1$ applications of *cut* using $\vdash A_i$ for $i = 1...j-1$ and $i = j+1...k$ as the first premise. Consequently, constraint 2b could not be violated for this rule instance. Therefore M is a $\mathcal{M}_r$ model and the assumption about G not being derivable in L_{cs} cannot be true. $\qquad\square$

Now suppose that KB rules are fuzzy and truth values greater or equal to h are associated with the rules. If the semantics of fuzzy KB rules is based on the residuum of the Godel t-norm [12], then this semantics can be expressed as follows: $|A_0| \geq \min\{|A_1|, ..., |A_k|, |A_0 \Leftarrow A_1 \wedge ... \wedge A_k|\}$. In the case of fuzzy KB rules, condition 2a in the definition of $\mathcal{M}_r$ models should be changed to the above inequality. Condition 2b remains unchanged.

Let $m'(\tau) = \min\{\min_{A \in \mathcal{F}} |A|, \min_{S \in \mathcal{R}} |S|\}$ where $\mathcal{F}$ is the set of non-obscure occurrences of ground KB fact instances in derivation τ and $\mathcal{R}$ is the set of KB rules occurring in τ as premises of *cut*. Clearly, the theorems 4.3 and 4.4 hold in the case of fuzzy KB rules if condition 2a in the definition of $\mathcal{M}_r$ models is changed as described earlier and if m is replaced by m'.

5 Related Work

An overview of KB inference methods including resolution-based methods can be found in [29]. Inference from non-Horn KBs without RAA is more powerful than forward or backward chaining and less powerful than FOL inference from non-Horn KBs. See [30] for a comparison of these inference mechanisms. Ordered resolution is recognized as one of the most efficient inference methods [3]. It is used in modern theorem provers [18]. Ordered resolution has been adapted to inference from non-Horn KBs without RAA [30].

Description logics [2] and other logics with more limited capabilities than FOL are relevant to KB inference. Inference without RAA is used in argumentation logics [16]. The proof theory suggested in that paper is natural deduction without the RAA rule. Other arumentation logics with limited inference capabilities have been proposed in [5].

Inference from fuzzy KBs is focused on numerical calculations approximating truth values. Forward chaining normally serves as the inference mechanism for fuzzy KBs [4]. Inference from fuzzy KBs may also involve fuzzification and defuzzification [4]. For non-Horn KBs with neural and evaluable predicates, symbolic inference is done first and then approximate truth values are computed by traversing the derivation trees. Instead of engaging fuzzy truth functions for all logical connectives [12], we utilize constraints imposed by KB rules on fuzzy truth values.

Paper [7] is a comprehensive survey of recent work in the area of neural-symbolic computing. Neural-symbolic systems integrate neural networks and inference methods. In particular, neural networks are used for guiding symbolic inference [34,14,27]. Integration of neural and fuzzy systems is analyzed in [1].

Paper [28] introduces a neural-symbolic method employing weighted real-valued functions for calculating lower and upper bounds of the truth values of

FOL formulas. Inference is implemented as alternating upward and downward passes over the structure of the formulas. Truth value bounds are adjusted during these passes. Modus Ponens and Modus Tollens are used to get truth value bounds. In our work, KB rules play the role of premises of Modus Ponens, and swapped KB rules can be viewed as premises of Modus Tollens.

Non-Horn KBs containing neural and evaluable predicates are similar to possibilistic logic [10] in the sense that in both of them, real numbers are associated with derived ground literals. A survey of fuzzy proof theories in which numbers indicating truthness are attached to FOL formulas is presented in [11]. The major difference of our approach is that literals are the only FOL formulas involved in the KB formalism considered here. Also, we use derivation trees as the input for calculating the truth values of derived literals.

ProbLog [26] extends Prolog by associating probabilities with facts. It is assumed that all ground instances of a non-ground fact are mutually independent and share the same probability. ProbLog engines calculate approximate probabilities for inference goals. Since Prolog has positive goals only, negation as failure is adopted in ProbLog to derive negative goals. Non-Horn KBs with neural and evaluable predicates are not probabilistic, they use constraints on the truth values of literals for getting lower bounds of the truth values of derived goals. Inference of negative goals from non-Horn KBs is direct, which helps avoid controversies related to negation as failure [8].

DeepProbLog [20] extends ProbLog by allowing neural networks to be associated with facts instead of probabilities. The probabilities of ground instances of a fact are calculated by the neural network associated with the respective predicate. This is similar to our assumption except for the interpretation of the values yielded by neural networks. We follow their traditional interpretation as fuzzy truth values of ground facts.

Sequent calculus derivations for Horn formulas are researched in [22]. Substructural sequent calculi have been investigated for decades [25,24]. L_{cs} instances are substructural calculi. The set of L_{cs} calculi is particularly tailored to inference from non-Horn KBs with neural and evaluable predicates. The replacement of the two negation rules with the swap rule makes L_{cs} single-succedent, which is essential for the approximation of truth values.

L_{cs} instances contain non-logical axioms which represent KB rules and facts. The cut rule is a core of these calculi. Properties of sequent calculi with non-logical axioms in the form of so-called mathematical basic sequents are investigated in [23]. Axioms corresponding to KB rules/facts can be transformed to mathematical basic sequents.

Like L_{cs}, LK_{-c} calculi from [31] contain non-logical axioms representing KB rules and facts. LK_{-c} calculi characterize inference of literals from non-Horn KBs without using RAA. Those calculi have the same inference power as L_{cs} but they employ standard negation rules as opposed to the swap rule, they allow multiple literals in succedents. LK_{-c} derivations cannot be directly used for the approximation of fuzzy truth values.

6 Conclusion

The language of non-Horn KBs is much simpler than the language of FOL. Negation is a connective in this language. Conjunction with a variable number of arguments and implication are embedded in KB rules but they are not standalone connectives in the language. Non-Horn KBs with evaluable and neural predicates integrate reasoning, computation, and neural networks. They are neural-symbolic systems [19] which fully integrate symbolic reasoning and neural networks implementing relations, that is, predicates. These KBs bear similarities with fuzzy KBs [4], but the inference is separated from numeric computations.

The calculi and models presented here are comprehensible. Both non-logical axioms of L_{cs} and the constraints in $\mathcal{M}_r$ models are projections of KB facts and rules. The most important feature of our characterization of non-Horn KBs with evaluable and neural predicates is that L_{cs} derivations provide sufficient information for the calculation of lower bounds of the truth values of the derivation goals. Hilbert-type systems are less adequate for characterizing these KBs because they would explicitly include other logical connectives, possibly non-standard ones.

It is feasible to get multiple L_{cs} derivations of the same goal. These derivations of one literal may give various approximations of the truth value of this literal. It may be beneficial to skip some facts with truth values close to h during the derivation process. The design of efficient inference methods capturing higher truth values is beyond the scope of this paper. Investigation of the applicability of other fuzzy truth functions [12] to non-Horn KBs containing neural and evaluable predicates is a topic for future research.

References

[1] Abraham, A., *Adaptation of fuzzy inference system using neural learning*, in: *Fuzzy systems engineering*, Springer, 2005 pp. 53–83.

[2] Baader, F., I. Horrocks and U. Sattler, *Description logics*, Foundations of Artificial Intelligence **3** (2008), pp. 135–179.

[3] Bachmair, L. and H. Ganzinger, *Resolution theorem proving*, in: *Handbook of automated reasoning*, Elsevier, 2001 pp. 19–99.

[4] Barros, L. C. d., R. C. Bassanezi and W. A. Lodwick, "A first course in fuzzy logic, fuzzy dynamical systems, and biomathematics: theory and applications," Springer, 2017.

[5] Besnard, P. and A. Hunter, *A review of argumentation based on deductive arguments*, Handbook of Formal Argumentation (2018), pp. 437–484.

[6] Chang, C.-L. and R. C.-T. Lee, "Symbolic logic and mechanical theorem proving," Academic press, 1973.

[7] d'Avila Garcez, A. S., M. Gori, L. C. Lamb, L. Serafini, M. Spranger and S. N. Tran, *Neural-symbolic computing: An effective methodology for principled integration of machine learning and reasoning*, Journal of Applied Logics **6** (2019), pp. 611–632.

[8] Denecker, M., M. Truszczynski and J. Vennekens, *About negation-as-failure and the informal semantics of logic programming*, Association for Logic Programming (2017).

[9] Dong, H., J. Mao, T. Lin, C. Wang, L. Li and D. Zhou, *Neural logic machines*, in: *International Conference on Learning Representations*, 2019.

[10] Dubois, D. and H. Prade, *Possibilistic logic-an overview.*, in: *Computational logic*, 2014, pp. 197–255.
[11] Gottwald, S., "A treatise on many-valued logics," Research Studies Press, 2001.
[12] Hájek, P., "Metamathematics of fuzzy logic," Springer Science & Business Media, 2013.
[13] Hong, J. and T. P. Pavlic, *An insect-inspired randomly, weighted neural network with random fourier features for neuro-symbolic relational learning*, in: *Neural-Symbolic Learning and Reasoning* (2021).
[14] Huang, D., P. Dhariwal, D. Song and I. Sutskever, *Gamepad: A learning environment for theorem proving*, in: *International Conference on Learning Representations*, 2019.
[15] Ishihara, T., K. Hayashi, H. Manabe, M. Shimbo and M. Nagata, *Neural tensor networks with diagonal slice matrices*, in: *Proceedings of the 2018 Conference of the North American Chapter of the Association for Computational Linguistics: Human Language Technologies, Volume 1 (Long Papers)*, 2018, pp. 506–515.
[16] Kakas, A. C., P. Mancarella and F. Toni, *On argumentation logic and propositional logic*, Studia Logica **106** (2018), pp. 237–279.
[17] Kazakov, Y., *A framework of refutational theorem proving for saturationbased decision procedures*, Technical report, Research Report MPI-I-2005-2-004, Max-Planck-Institut für Informatik (2005).
[18] Kovács, L. and A. Voronkov, *First-order theorem proving and vampire*, in: *International Conference on Computer Aided Verification*, Springer, 2013, pp. 1–35.
[19] Lamb, L. C., A. S. d'Avila Garcez, M. Gori, M. O. R. Prates, P. H. C. Avelar and M. Y. Vardi, *Graph neural networks meet neural-symbolic computing: A survey and perspective*, in: *Proceedings of the Twenty-Ninth International Joint Conference on Artificial Intelligence*, 2020, pp. 4877–4884.
[20] Manhaeve, R., S. Dumančić, A. Kimmig, T. Demeester and L. De Raedt, *Neural probabilistic logic programming in deepproblog*, Artificial Intelligence **298** (2021), p. 103504.
[21] McCune, W., *Otter 3.3 reference manual and guide*, Technical report, Argonne National Lab. (2003).
[22] Miller, D., G. Nadathur, F. Pfenning and A. Scedrov, *Uniform proofs as a foundation for logic programming*, Annals of Pure and Applied logic **51** (1991), pp. 125–157.
[23] Negri, S. and J. Von Plato, "Structural proof theory," Cambridge University Press, 2001.
[24] Ono, H., *Logics without the contraction rule and residuated lattices*, Australasian Journal of Logic (2010).
[25] Paoli, F., "Substructural logics: a primer," Springer Science & Business Media, 2013.
[26] Raedt, L. D. and A. Kimmig, *Probabilistic (logic) programming concepts*, Machine Learning **100** (2015), pp. 5–47.
[27] Rawson, M. and G. Reger, *A neurally-guided, parallel theorem prover*, in: *International Symposium on Frontiers of Combining Systems*, Springer, 2019, pp. 40–56.
[28] Riegel, R., A. Gray, F. Luus, N. Khan, N. Makondo, I. Y. Akhalwaya, H. Qian, R. Fagin, F. Barahona, U. Sharma et al., *Logical neural networks*, arXiv preprint arXiv:2006.13155 (2020).
[29] Russell, S. and P. Norvig, "Artificial Intelligence: A Modern Approach," Prentice Hall Press, 2009, 3rd edition.
[30] Sakharov, A., *Inference methods for evaluable knowledge bases*, in: *Software Engineering Application in Informatics*, Lecture Notes in Networks and Systems (2021), pp. 499–510.
[31] Sakharov, A., *A logical characterization of evaluable knowledge bases*, in: *14th International Conference on Agents and Artificial Intelligence*, 2022, pp. 681–688.
[32] Santoro, A., D. Raposo, D. G. Barrett, M. Malinowski, R. Pascanu, P. Battaglia and T. Lillicrap, *A simple neural network module for relational reasoning*, Advances in neural information processing systems **30** (2017).
[33] Serafini, L. and A. S. d'Avila Garcez, *Logic tensor networks: Deep learning and logical reasoning from data and knowledge*, in: *Neural-Symbolic Learning and Reasoning* (2016).
[34] Wang, M., Y. Tang, J. Wang and J. Deng, *Premise selection for theorem proving by deep graph embedding*, Advances in neural information processing systems **30** (2017).

Experiments in Kratzer Modal Semantics Using Isabelle/HOL

Ali Farjami

Iran University of Science and Technology
farjami110@gmail.com

Abstract

Benzmüller, Parent and van der Torre introduced the LogiKEy methodology for the formalization and automation of new ethical reasoners, normative theories and deontic logics. This article uses LogiKEy to experiment and compare Åqvist preference models with Kratzer models for conditional obligations.

Keywords: LogiKEy methodology, Kratzer deontic models, Åqvist preference models.

1 Introduction

In order to design and expriment in normative theories, Benzmüller, Parent and van der Torre introduced the LogiKEy methodology, based on the semantical embedding of deontic logics into classic higher-order logic. Earlier work presented semantical embedding of two traditions in deontic logic in the LogiKEy framework, namely Åqvist's dyadic deontic logic **E** [3] and Makinson and van der Torre's input/output (I/O) logic [2,4]. Subsequent work provided the Isabelle/HOL dataset for the LogiKEy workbench [1].

This article uses the LogiKEy methodology to experiment and compare Åqvist preference models with Kratzer models for conditional obligations. Horty [5] compared Kratzer deontic models with standard deontic models (SDL) and van Fraassen models [8]. Comparison of the Kratzerian framework with other well-known deontic models such as Åqvist preference models is open.

The article is structured as follows. Section 2 collects basic definitions of Åqvist preference models and Kratzer models. The semantical embedding of Kratzer models in HOL is then devised and studied in Section 3. This section also compares Åqvist preference models and Kratzer models for conditional obligations. Section 4 concludes the paper.

2 Preliminaries

Syntax The language, for the purpose of this paper, is obtained by adding the $\bigcirc$ operator (for monadic obligation) and $\bigcirc(\_/\_)$ operator (for conditional

36

obligation) to the language of propositional logic. $\bigcirc \varphi$ is read "φ is obligatory" and $\bigcirc(\psi/\varphi)$ is read "If φ, then ψ is obligatory". The set of well-formed formulas (wffs) is defined in the straightforward way.

Semantics (Åqvist preference model) A preference model is a structure $M = \langle W, \succeq, V \rangle$ where:

- W is a non-empty set of possible worlds (W is called "universe");
- $\succeq \subseteq W \times W$ (intuitively, $\succeq$ is a betterness or comparative goodness relation; "$s \succeq t$" can be read as "world s is at least as good as world t");
- V is a function assigning to each atomic wff a set of worlds, i.e., $V(p) \subseteq W$ (intuitively, $V(p)$ is the set of worlds at which p is true).

No specific properties (like reflexivity or transitivity) are required for the betterness relation. Given a preference model $M = \langle W, \succeq, V \rangle$ and a world $s \in W$, the satisfaction relation $M, s \vDash \varphi$ (read as "world s satisfies φ in model M") is defined by induction on the structure of φ as described below. Intuitively, the evaluation rule for the dyadic obligation operator puts $\bigcirc(\psi/\varphi)$ true whenever all the best φ-worlds are ψ-worlds. Here, best is defined in terms of optimality rather than maximality [7]. A φ-world is optimal if it is at least as good as any other φ-world. We define $V^M(\varphi) = \{s \in W \mid M, s \vDash \varphi\}$ and $\mathrm{opt}_{\succeq}(V^M(\varphi)) = \{s \in V^M(\varphi) \mid \forall t(t \vDash \varphi \to s \succeq t)\}$. Whenever the model M is obvious from context, we write $V(\varphi)$ instead of $V^M(\varphi)$.

$$M, s \vDash p \text{ if and only if } s \in V(p)$$
$$M, s \vDash \neg\varphi \text{ if and only if } M, s \nvDash \varphi \text{ (that is, not } M, s \vDash \varphi)$$
$$M, s \vDash \varphi \vee \psi \text{ if and only if } M, s \vDash \varphi \text{ or } M, s \vDash \psi$$
$$M, s \vDash \bigcirc(\psi/\varphi) \text{ if and only if } \mathrm{opt}_{\succeq}(V(\varphi)) \subseteq V(\psi)$$

As usual, a formula φ is valid in a preference model $M = \langle W, \succeq, V \rangle$ (notation: $M \vDash \varphi$) if and only if, for all worlds $s \in W$, $M, s \vDash \varphi$. A formula φ is valid (notation: $\vDash \varphi$) if and only if it is valid in every preference model. The notions of semantic consequence and satisfiability in a model are defined as usual. Åqvist dyadic deontic logic system **E** [7] is sound and complete with respect to the class of all preference models.

Semantics (Kratzer's model KD) A Kratzer model is a structure $M = \langle W, f, g, v \rangle$, where f and g are functions from worlds to set of propositions. f is the modal base function, and g is the ordering source function. g ranks the worlds as follows:

$$s \succeq_{g(w)} t \text{ iff, for all } X \in g(w), \text{ if } t \in X, \text{ then } s \in X.$$
$$(s \succ_{g(w)} t \text{ iff } s \succeq_{g(w)} t \text{ and } t \nsucceq_{g(w)} s)$$

Best worlds are defined as usual: $Best_{g(w)}(X) = \{s \in X : \neg\exists t \in X \ (t \succ_{g(w)} s)\}$. In this article, Kratzer models are restricted to models with the stoppered property, a form of the limit assumption. A Kratzer model is stoppered if and only if for all w if $s \in \bigcap f(w)$ then $s \in Best_{g(w)}(\bigcap f(w))$ or $\exists t . t \in Best_{g(w)}(\bigcap f(w)) \wedge t \succeq_{g(w)} s$ (moreover, we can add the consistency condition $\bigcap f(w) \neq \emptyset$).

The satisfaction relation for the monadic obligation [5] is defined as follows:

$$M, w \models_{KD} \bigcirc \varphi \quad \text{if and only if} \quad Best_{g(w)}(\bigcap f(w)) \subseteq V(\varphi)$$

and the dyadic obligation [5] as follows:

$$M, w \models_{KD} \bigcirc(\psi/\varphi) \quad \text{if and only if} \quad Best_{g(w)}(V(\varphi) \cap \bigcap f(w)) \subseteq V(\psi)$$

See Fact 2 and Fact 3 [5] for the connection between Kratzer's model KD and stadard deontic models.

3 Implementation and Experiments

The semantical embedding of Kratzer models in HOL is similar to Åqvist preference models. See the previous work [3] for the implementation and experiment of Åqvist preference models in Isabelle/HOL.

3.1 Kratzer models in HOL

Kratzer's system logical operators are implemented in Isabelle/HOL (cf. Fig. 1).

- On line 2, the type i for possible words is introduced.
- On line 3, the type τ for formulas is introduced.
- On line 3, a designated constant for the actual world (aw) is introduced.
- Lines 4–10 define the Boolean connectives in the usual way.
- On line 12, the constants f and g are introduced. f encodes the modal base function and g the ordering source.
- Lines 14 – 17 define the ordering $\succeq_{g(w)}$ (and $\succ_{g(w)}$).
- On line 19, the factual background $\bigcap f(w)$ in a world w is introduced.

```
1 theory  Unification_Problem  imports Main
2 begin  typedecl i — ‹type for possible worlds›
3 type_synonym τ = "(i⇒bool)"  consts  aw::i (* actual world *)
4 definition ddetop          :: "τ" ("⊤")        where "⊤ ≡ λw. True"
5 definition ddebot          :: "τ" ("⊥")        where "⊥ ≡ λw. False"
6 definition ddeneg          :: "τ⇒τ" ("¬_"[52]53)  where "¬φ ≡ λw. ¬φ(w)"
7 definition ddeand          :: "τ⇒τ⇒τ" (infixr"∧"51) where "φ∧ψ ≡ λw. φ(w)∧ψ(w)"
8 definition ddeor           :: "τ⇒τ⇒τ" (infixr"∨"50) where "φ∨ψ ≡ λw. φ(w)∨ψ(w)"
9 definition ddeimp          :: "τ⇒τ⇒τ" (infixr"→"49) where "φ→ψ ≡ λw. φ(w)⟶ψ(w)"
10 definition ddeequivt      :: "τ⇒τ⇒τ" (infixr"↔"48) where "φ↔ψ ≡ λw. φ(w)⟷ψ(w)"
11
12 consts f:: "i⇒((i⇒bool)⇒bool)"  consts g:: "i⇒((i⇒bool)⇒bool)"
13
14 definition  mmodalrelation  :: "i⇒i⇒i⇒bool" (infix "≽g<_>" 53)
15   where "s ≽g<w> t ≡ ∀X.(g w X ⟶ (X t ⟶ X s))"
16 definition  mmodalrelations :: "i⇒i⇒i⇒bool" (infix "≻g<_>" 54)
17   where "s ≻g<w> t  ≡ (s ≽g<w> t) ∧ ¬(t ≽g<w> s)"
18
19 definition preferelation :: "i⇒τ" ("⋂f<_>"[9]110) where "⋂f<w> ≡ λs. ∀X. (f w X ⟶ X s)"
```

Fig. 1. Kratzer models in Isabelle/HOL

Kratzer monadic and dyadic deontic operators are defined in HOL and consequently in Isabelle/HOL (cf. Fig. 2).

- Lines 21 – 22, Best worlds are defined based on the ordering source $g(w)$.
- Lines 24 – 26 define stoppered property.
- Lines 28 – 29, the monadic obligation operator is defined.
- On line 31, the infex operator $\cap$ operator is introduced.
- Lines 33 – 34, the dyadic obligation operator is defined.

```
21 definition Bestfunction ::"i⇒τ⇒τ" ("Bestg<_><_>")
22   where "Bestg<w><X> ≡ λs. (X s ∧ ¬(∃t. (X t ∧ (t ≻g<w> s))))"
23
24 axiomatization where
25 stoppered : "∀w.
26 ∀s.((⋂f<w> ) s  ⟶  ((Bestg<w><( ⋂f<w> )> )(s) ∨ (∃t. (Bestg<w><( ⋂f<w> )> )(t) ∧ t ≽g<w> s)))"
27
28 definition Kratzobliga :: "τ⇒τ" ("○ᵏᶜ")
29   where "○ᵏᶜφ ≡ λw. (∀s. ((Bestg<w><( ⋂f<w> ) > )(s)  ⟶  (φ)(s) ))"
30
31 abbreviation(input) msubintert :: "τ⇒τ⇒τ" (infix "∩" 54) where "φ ∩ ψ ≡λX. φ X ∧ ψ X"
32
33 definition kratzdyadic :: "τ⇒τ⇒τ" ("○ᵏᶜ<_|_>")
34   where "○ᵏᶜ<v|φ> ≡ λw. (∀s. ((Bestg<w>< (( ⋂f<w> ) ∩ (v)) > )(s)  ⟶  (φ)(s) ))"
```

Fig. 2. Monadic and dyadic obligations in Isabelle/HOL

3.2   Åqvist Preference models $\Rightarrow$ Kratzer models

For translating the preference models $\langle W, \succeq, V \rangle$ to Kratzer models $\langle W, f, g, v \rangle$ the modal base and ordering source are defined as follows (cf. Fig. 3):

- The modal base for the current world is defined as the most preferable accessible worlds i.e. $\bigcap f(w) = \text{opt}_{\succeq}(R(w))$. It is used the abbreviation $R(w) = \{s | s \succeq w\}$.
- It is used in two ways for defining the ordering sources:
  - Normality source: $g_n(w) = \{X : \text{opt}_{\succeq}(R(w)) \subseteq X\}$
  - Practicality source: $g_p(w) = \{X : \text{opt}_{\succeq}(R(w)) \cap X \neq \emptyset\}$

The translation is non-trivial, since the modal base function is not empty; and it is different from the Lewis's translation of ordering semantics to premise semantics [6]. The model translation characterizes Åqvist preference models [7] within the Kratzerian framework for conditional obligation.

- On line 35, the modal base $\bigcap f$ is defined.
- On line 37, the normality ordering source $g_n(w)$ is defined.
- On line 38, the practicality ordering source $g_p(w)$ is defined.
- Lines 40 – 43, define the normality ranking relation $\succeq_{g_n(w)}$ (and $\succ_{g_n(w)}$).
- Lines 45 – 48, define the practicality ranking relation $\succeq_{g_p(w)}$ (and $\succ_{g_p(w)}$).

```
35  definition preferelation :: "i⇒τ" ( "⋂f<_>"[9]110) where "⋂f<w> ≡ λs. opt<R w> s"
36
37  definition normalitysource :: "i⇒τ⇒bool " ("gn<_>") where "gn<w> ≡ λX. opt<R w> ⊆ X"
38  definition practicalsource :: "i⇒τ⇒bool " ("gp<_>") where "gp<w> ≡ λX. (∃s. opt꜀R w> s ∧ X s)"
39
40  definition nmmodalrelation   :: "i⇒i⇒i⇒bool" (infix "≽gn<_>" 53)
41    where "s ≽gn<w> t ≡ ∀X. (gn<w> X ⟶ (X t ⟶X s))"
42  definition nmmodalrelations  :: "i⇒i⇒i⇒bool" (infix "≻gn<_>" 54)
43    where "s ≻gn<w> t ≡ (s ≽gn<w> t) ∧ ¬(t ≽gn<w> s)"
44
45  definition pmmodalrelation  :: "i⇒i⇒i⇒bool" (infix "≽gp<_>" 53)
46    where "s ≽gp<w> t ≡ ∀X. (gp<w> X ⟶ (X t ⟶X s))"
47  definition pmmodalrelations  :: "i⇒i⇒1⇒bool" (infix "≻gp<_>" 54)
48    where "s ≻gp<w> t ≡ (s ≽gp<w> t) ∧ ¬(t ≽gp<w> s)"
```

Fig. 3. Normality and practicality ordering sources in Isabelle/HOL

Two different monadic and dyadic deontic operators are defined based on the two mentioned ordering sources and the modal base (cf. Fig. 4).

- Lines 50 – 53, define Best worlds based on the normality ordering source $g_n(w)$ and practicality ordering source $\succeq_{g_p(w)}$.
- Lines 55 – 60, define stoppered property for the normality and practicality ordering sources.
- Lines 62 – 65, define monadic obligation operators based on the normality and practicality ordering sources.
- Lines 67 – 70, define dyadic obligation operators based on the normality and practicality ordering sources.

```
50  definition BestfunctionN ::"i⇒τ⇒τ" ("Bestgn<_><_>")
51    where "Bestgn<w><X> ≡ λs. (X s ∧ ¬(∃t. (X t ∧ (t ≻gn<w> s))))"
52  definition BestfunctionP ::"i⇒τ⇒τ" ("Bestgp<_><_>")
53    where "Bestgp<w><X> ≡ λs. (X s ∧ ¬(∃t. (X t ∧ (t ≻gp<w> s))))"
54
55  axiomatization where
56  stopperedN : " ∀w. ∀s.
57  ((⋂f<w> ) s ⟶ ((Bestgn<w>< ( ⋂f<w> ) > )(s) ∨ (∃t. (Bestgn<w>< ( ⋂f<w> ) > )(t) ∧ t ≽gn<w> s)))"
58  and
59  stopperedP : " ∀w. ∀s.
60  ((⋂f<w> ) s ⟶ ((Bestgp<w>< ( ⋂f<w> ) > )(s) ∨ (∃t. (Bestgp<w>< ( ⋂f<w> ) > )(t) ∧ t ≽gp<w> s)))"
61
62  definition KratzobligaN : "τ⇒τ" ("○ᵏᶜⁿ")
63    where "○ᵏᶜⁿ φ ≡ λw. (∀s. ((Bestgn<w>< ( ⋂f<w> ) > )(s) ⟶ (φ)(s) ))"
64  definition KratzobligaP : "τ⇒τ" ("○ᵏᶜᵖ")
65    where "○ᵏᶜᵖφ ≡ λw. (∀s. ((Bestgp<w>< ( ⋂f<w> ) > )(s) ⟶ (φ)(s) ))"
66
67  definition kratzdyadicN : "τ⇒τ⇒τ" ("○ᵏᶜⁿ<_|_>")
68    where "○ᵏᶜⁿ<ᵥ|ᵩ> ≡ λw. (∀s. ((Bestgn<w>< ((⋂f<w> ) ∩ (φ) > )(s) ⟶ (ψ)(s) ))"
69  definition kratzdyadicP : "τ⇒τ⇒τ" ("○ᵏᶜᵖ<_|_>")
70    where "○ᵏᶜᵖ<ᵥ|ᵩ> ≡ λw. (∀s. ((Bestgp<w>< ((⋂f<w> ) ∩ (φ) > )(s) ⟶ (ψ)(s) ))"
```

Fig. 4. Deontic operators based on the normality/practicality sources in Isabelle/HOL

3.3   Results

Isabelle/HOL shows that the dyadic operator defined in Åqvist Preference models, when the condition is restricted by the modal base or factual backgrounds $\bigcap f(aw)$, is equal to the both newly introduced dyadic operators in Kratzer models ($\lfloor\ \rfloor_?$ denotes satisfaction in the actual world (aw)) (cf. Fig. 5).

```
lemma "⌊○<ψ|φ∧⋂f<aw> > → (○ᵏᶜⁿ<ψ|φ> )⌋₁"
  by (simp add: BestfunctionN_def ddeactual_def ddeand_def ddecond_def ddeimp_def ddeopt_def
kratzdyadicN_def preferelation_def)
lemma "⌊○<ψ|φ∧⋂f<aw> > → (○ᵏᶜᵖ<ψ|φ> )⌋₁"
  by (simp add: BestfunctionP_def ddeactual_def ddeand_def ddecond_def ddeimp_def ddeopt_def
kratzdyadicP_def preferelation_def)
lemma "⌊(○ᵏᶜⁿ<ψ|φ> ) → ○<ψ|φ∧⋂f<aw> >⌋₁"
  by (smt BestfunctionN_def ddeactual_def ddeand_def ddecond_def ddeimp_def ddeopt_def
kratzdyadicN_def nmmodalrelation_def nmmodalrelations_def normalitysource_def preferelation_def)
lemma "⌊(○ᵏᶜᵖ<ψ|φ> ) → ○<ψ|φ∧⋂f<aw> >⌋₁"
  by (smt BestfunctionP_def ddeactual_def ddeand_def ddecond_def ddeimp_def ddeopt_def
kratzdyadicP_def pmmodalrelation_def pmmodalrelations_def practicalsource_def preferelation_def)
```

Fig. 5. Conditional obligations in Åqvist preference models and Kratzer models

The experiments show that the following semantical relations holds, for a given preference model and the two mentioned translated Kratzer models.

$$\mathrm{opt}_{\succeq}(V(\varphi) \cap \bigcap f(aw)) \subseteq V(\psi) \iff Best_{g_n(aw)}(V(\varphi) \cap \bigcap f(aw)) \subseteq V(\psi)$$
$$\mathrm{opt}_{\succeq}(V(\varphi) \cap \bigcap f(aw)) \subseteq V(\psi) \iff Best_{g_p(aw)}(V(\varphi) \cap \bigcap f(aw)) \subseteq V(\psi)$$

Hence, it is derived the semantical relation between normality and practicality ordering sources based on the given preference relation as follows:

$$Best_{g_n(aw)}(V(\varphi) \cap \mathrm{opt}_{\succeq}(\succeq (aw))) \subseteq V(\psi)$$
$$\Updownarrow$$
$$Best_{g_p(aw)}(V(\varphi) \cap \mathrm{opt}_{\succeq}(\succeq (aw))) \subseteq V(\psi)$$

4   Conclusions

The shallow semantical embedding of Kratzer models in higher-order logic is presented. The LogiKEy methodology is used to compare conditional obligation operators in Åqvist preference models and Kratzer models. It is interesting to provide a mathematical explanation for this comparison.

Correspondence between ordering semantics and premise semantics is shown by Lewis [6]. The experiments in this article aim to extend Lewis results for decomposing a preference relation to a two-component premise semantics (modal base + ordering source). The experiments could investigate a bridge between preference aggregation in computational social choice theory and conditionals in Linguistics.

Acknowledgements

I thank anonymous reviewers for valuable comments.

References

[1] Benzmüller, C., A. Farjami, D. Fuenmayor, P. Meder, X. Parent, A. Steen, L. van der Torre and V. Zahoransky, *LogiKEy workbench: Deontic logics, logic combinations and expressive*

ethical and legal reasoning (Isabelle/HOL dataset), Data in Brief (2020), pp. 1–15.

[2] Benzmüller, C., A. Farjami, P. Meder and X. Parent, *I/O logic in HOL*, Journal of Applied Logics – IfCoLoG Journal of Logics and their Applications (Special Issue on Reasoning for Legal AI) **6** (2019), pp. 715–732.

[3] Benzmüller, C., A. Farjami and X. Parent, *Åqvist's dyadic deontic logic E in HOL*, Journal of Applied Logics – IfCoLoG Journal of Logics and their Applications (Special Issue on Reasoning for Legal AI) **6** (2019), pp. 733–755.

[4] Farjami, A., "Discursive Input/Output Logic: Deontic Modals, and Computation," Ph.D. thesis, University of Luxembourg, Luxembourg (2020).

[5] Horty, J., *Deontic modals: Why abandon the classical semantics?*, Pacific Philosophical Quarterly **95** (2014), pp. 424–460.

[6] Lewis, D., *Ordering semantics and premise semantics for counterfactuals*, Journal of Philosophical Logic **10** (1981), pp. 217–234.

[7] Parent, X., *Completeness of Åqvist's systems E and F*, The Review of Symbolic Logic **8** (2015), pp. 164–177.

[8] van Fraassen, B. C., *The logic of conditional obligation*, Journal of Philosophical Logic **1** (1972), pp. 417–438.

Epistemic Logics over Weighted Graphs

Xiaolong Liang

Department of Philosophy (Zhuhai)
Sun Yat-sen University
Zhuhai, P.R. China
lianghillon@gmail.com

Yì N. Wáng [1]

Department of Philosophy (Zhuhai)
Sun Yat-sen University
Zhuhai, P.R. China
ynw@xixilogic.org

Abstract

In this paper we introduce weighted graphs and as a special case of it, similarity graphs, which can be used to model similarity between epistemic objects. We study epistemic logics interpreted over weighted models, their correspondence to classical epistemic logics, sound and complete axiomatizations, as well as the computational complexity results for the validity and model checking problems.

Keywords: epistemic logic, weighted model, similarity model, correspondence, completeness, complexity.

1 Introduction

While similarity is a notion closely related to knowledge, it has not played an important role or been explicitly involved in the classical representation of knowledge in the area of epistemic logic [9,6,11]. In recent years, there have been studies and developments in this area in the relationship between them [5,12]. The technical framework can be traced back to that of weighted modal logics [10,8].

In this paper, we borrow the notion of similarity from the area of data mining, where it is mainly introduced to measure the alikeness of two data objects. While in data mining, distance and similarity measures are typically concrete algorithms designed for concrete scenarios, such as distance and similarity between matrices, texts, graphs, etc. (see e.g. [1, Chapter 3]), there is literature defining general properties of distance and similarity measures. For instance,

---
[1] Corresponding author. The author acknowledges funding support by the National Social Science Fund of China (Grant No. 20&ZD047).

in [13], it writes that the following properties typically hold for $s(x, y)$ – the similarity between points x and y – which is a binary numerical function from two data objects to the range $[0, 1]$:

- Positivity: $s(x, y) = 1$ only if $x = y$;
- Symmetry: $s(x, y) = s(y, x)$ (for all x and y).

Yet we are not ultimately interested in the measures of similarity, but rather modeling it and derive from it the notion of knowledge. We achieve this by interpreting knowledge with a type of models which we call *weighted models* (and a special type of it called *similarity models*). Intuitively, "a knows φ" ($K_a\varphi$) is understood as "φ is true in all states that look similar in a's eyes to the factual state". A "state" here can be understood as a data object which is the focus of data mining, but can also be regarded as any epistemic object, possible situation, etc. We generalize the similarity function by replacing its range $[0, 1]$ with an arbitrary set of epistemic abilities. In our settings, the degrees of similarity may not be compared or ordered.

We study epistemic logics interpreted over weighted models and similarity models. Correspondence is found between these logics and the classical multi-modal logic K_m and KB_m, respectively. Then the classical axiomatization for K_m (and KB_m respectively) becomes an axiomatization for its correspondent in this paper as well. The soundness and completeness of the axiomatizations, and the validity problem for these logics, are therefore achieved via the correspondence. We show in addition that the model checking problem for these logics are in P.

Our work is different from the recent developments of epistemic logics interpreted via the notions of similarity/distance, e.g., [5,12], also in that we use the standard language of epistemic logic, while the other solutions usually make explicit use of the degree of (dis)similiarity in the language (e.g., with a sentence $K_a^r\varphi$ meaning "a knows φ under the strength of effort or confidence r").

The structure of the paper is as follows. We introduce and illustrate weighted graphs and similarity graphs in Section 2. Epistemic logic over weighted models (ELW) is introduced in Section 3, in which we study the correspondence of the logic to the classical epistemic logic, a sound and complete axiomatization for ELW, and the computational complexity results of the validity and model checking problems for ELW. We study similar problems for epistemic logic over similarity models (ELS). We conclude in the last section.

2   Weighted Graphs

In this section we introduce two types of *weighted graphs*, in which weights are intended to stand for the areas of similarity/uncertainty between epistemic objects – such as data, areas of interest, etc. – which are characterized by nodes of the graphs. Weighted graphs will be used in the next section for interpreting the classical epistemic language.

Definition 2.1 A *weighted graph* is a pair (W, A, E), where

- W is a nonempty set of states or nodes, called the *domain*;
- A is an arbitrary set of abstract epistemic abilities, which can be empty, finite or infinite depending on the context;
- $E : W \times W \to \wp(A)$, called an *edge function*, maps every pair of states to a set of epistemic abilities, meaning the two states are indistinguishable for persons with only these epistemic abilities.

Here we adopt a very general definition of epistemic abilities which are not necessarily (though possibly) ordered.

Definition 2.2 A weighted graph (W, A, E) is called a *similarity graph* if the following hold for all $s, t \in W$:

(i) Positivity: $E(s, t) = A$ implies $s = t$, and

(ii) Symmetry: $E(s, t) = E(t, s)$.

In the above definition, the edge function E is treated as presenting the *similarity relation* between the states. Similarities are treated to be *objective* here, in the sense that it does not change per agent. The conditions *positivity* and *symmetry* are generalizations of typical ones for characterizing similarity between data objects (cf. e.g., [13]).[2]

Example 2.3 Three authors work together on a paper that consists of four main parts, the introductory and motivational part (e_1), introducing and defining new logics (e_2), axiomatizing the logics (e_3) and calculating complexity of the logics (e_4). The authors hold different opinions towards the presentation of the paper, and are bad at synchronizing their work. As a result, five variants of the paper, $s_1, s_2, \ldots, s_5$, come out during the process of collaboration. Having different texts does not necessarily lead two variants being really different – they may mean similarly, but may also have subtle and/or essential differences.
  Consider a situation that:

- Variants s_1, s_2, s_3 and s_5 are essentially the same in the part e_1, while s_4 is different in this part;
- Variants s_1 and s_3 are essentially the same in the parts e_2 and e_3, while s_2, s_4 and s_5, being the same also in the two parts, have differences from s_1 and s_3 in each of the two parts;
- s_1, s_2 and s_3 are essentially the same in e_4, but are different from s_4 and s_5 which keep the same in e_4.

The situation in Example 2.3 can be formalized with the similarity graph $G = (W, A, E)$, where:

- $W = \{s_1, s_2, s_3, s_4, s_5\}$;

---

[2] An implicit condition that is typically presumed is the converse of positivity, i.e., $E(s, t) = A$ if $s = t$. This will give us reflexivity of the graphs, which can be characterized by the valid sentences T ($K_a \varphi \to \varphi$). We leave this condition out of the paper as it is not put forward explicitly in the literature.

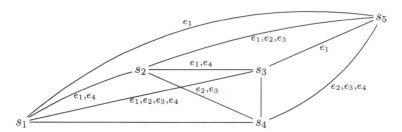

Fig. 1. Illustration of a similarity graph for Example 2.3. Reflexive edges are all omitted.

- $A = \{e_1, e_2, e_3, e_4\}$;
- E is such that $E(s_1, s_2) = E(s_2, s_3) = \{e_1, e_4\}$, $E(s_1, s_3) = \{e_1, e_2, e_3, e_4\}$, $E(s_1, s_4) = E(s_3, s_4) = \emptyset$, $E(s_1, s_5) = \{e_1\}$, $E(s_2, s_4) = \{e_2, e_3\}$, $E(s_2, s_5) = \{e_1, e_2, e_3\}$, $E(s_3, s_5) = \{e_1\}$, $E(s_4, s_5) = \{e_2, e_3, e_4\}$, and is reflexive (i.e., for all $x \in W$, $E(x, x) = A$) and symmetric (i.e., for all $x, y \in W$, $E(x, y) = E(y, x)$).

The similarity graph G is illustrated in Figure 1 in a usual way.

3 Epistemic Logic over Weighted Models (ELW)

In this section we introduce the minimal epistemic logic over weighted models (ELW). We show that there are reductions between ELW and the standard multimodal logic K_m. As a result, the standard axiomatization $\mathbf{K_m}$ for K_m is a sound and complete axiomatization for ELW as well. We also show that the validity problem for ELW is PSPACE complete and the model checking problem for ELW is in P.

3.1 Syntax and semantics

The language we use is the standard language of multi-agent epistemic logic [6,11]. Let Prop be a countable set of propositional variables and Ag a finite set of agents. These will be the default setting throughout the paper.

Definition 3.1 The formulas of the default language is given inductively as follows:

$$\varphi ::= p \mid \neg\varphi \mid (\varphi \rightarrow \varphi) \mid K_a\varphi$$

where $p \in$ Prop and $a \in$ Ag. Other boolean connectives, such as conjunction ($\wedge$), disjunction ($\vee$) and equivalence ($\leftrightarrow$) are treated as defined operators in a usual way. $K_a\varphi$ is intended to stand for "agent a knows φ".

We shall interpret the language using *weighted models*, which is a quintuple (W, A, E, C, ν) such that:

- (W, A, E) forms a weighted graph,
- $C : \text{Ag} \rightarrow \wp(A)$ assigns every agent a set of epistemic abilities it obtains, and
- $\nu : W \rightarrow \wp(\text{Prop})$ a valuation that assigns every state a set of propositional variables that are true in it.

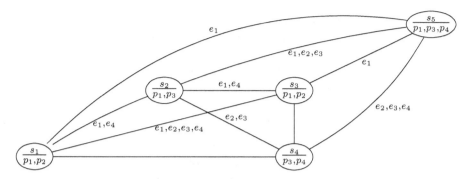

Fig. 2. Illustration of a weighted model (similarity model) for Example 3.2.

Example 3.2 (Continuation of Example 2.3) The three authors are named a, b and c. Author a is good at coming up with new ideas (e_1), introducing and defining new logics (e_2) and axiomatizing logics (e_3). Author b has expertise in e_2, e_3 and calculating complexity of logics e_4. Author c is good at e_4 only. It is important for the authors to verify whether the paper truly presents what they have planned to write, but it is hard for each of them to make a judgment for the parts outside their areas of expertise. Four propositions, p_1, p_2, p_3 and p_4, represent that the parts e_1 to e_4 properly put forward the planned content, respectively.

The fact is that the introductory section (e_1) and the introduction of logics (e_2) of the variants s_1 and s_3 are well written – truly presents the expected content. Also well written are the parts e_1 and e_3 of s_2, the parts e_3 and e_4 of s_4, and the parts e_1, e_3 and e_4 of s_5. The rest contain mispresentations.

Example 3.2 can be formalized in the weighted model (in fact, a *similarity model* which we will study in Section 4) $M = (W, A, E, C, \nu)$ where:

- (W, A, E) form the similarity graph presented below Example 2.3;
- C is such that $C(a) = \{e_1, e_2, e_3\}$, $C(b) = \{e_2, e_3, e_4\}$ and $C(c) = \{e_4\}$;
- ν is such that $\nu(s_1) = \nu(s_3) = \{p_1, p_2\}$, $\nu(s_2) = \{p_1, p_3\}$, $\nu(s_4) = \{p_3, p_4\}$ and $\nu(s_5) = \{p_1, p_3, p_4\}$.

Figure 2 illustrates the weighted model M introduced above.

Satisfaction of formulas in a weighted model is given as follows.

Definition 3.3 Given a formula φ, a weighted model $M = (W, A, E, C, \nu)$ and a state $s \in W$, we say φ is true or satisfied at s in M, denoted $M, s \models \varphi$, if the following recursive conditions are met:

$$
\begin{aligned}
M, s &\models p & &\Longleftrightarrow & &p \in \nu(s) \\
M, s &\models \neg\psi & &\Longleftrightarrow & &\text{not } M, s \models \psi \\
M, s &\models (\psi \wedge \chi) & &\Longleftrightarrow & &M, s \models \psi \text{ and } M, s \models \chi \\
M, s &\models K_a\psi & &\Longleftrightarrow & &\text{for all } t \in W, \text{ if } C(a) \subseteq E(s, t) \text{ then } M, t \models \psi.
\end{aligned}
$$

In the above definition, the interpretation of $K_a\psi$ includes a condition "$C(a) \subseteq E(s, t)$" which intuitively means that "agent a, with his abilities, cannot discern between the states s and t". So the formula $K_a \psi$ intuitively says that ψ is true in all states t that a cannot discern (between t and the factual state s).

In Example 3.2, we have the following truths:

- $M, s_2 \models K_a p_3$, meaning that when the variant s_2 is at hand, a knows that its third part (e_3) is well written.

- $M, s_4 \models \neg K_b p_1 \wedge \neg K_b \neg p_1$. When b sees the variant s_4, he does not know whether its introductory section (e_1) is well written.

- $M, s_3 \models K_c(K_a p_3 \vee K_a \neg p_3)$. When c proofreads the paper s_3, she knows that a knows whether its third part is well written.

Moreover, it is also possible to verify global truths at the model level:

- $M \models (K_a p_1 \vee K_a \neg p_1) \wedge (K_a p_2 \vee K_a \neg p_2) \wedge (K_a p_3 \vee K_a \neg p_3)$. No matter which variant the author a sees, he always knows whether its first three parts are well written.

A formula is called *valid* if and only if it is satisfied at all states of all weighted models. We refer to the resulting logic *epistemic logic over weighted models* (ELW for short).

3.2   Correspondence and completeness

We assume familiarity with standard multi-agent epistemic logic interpreted over *relational models* (a.k.a. *Kripke models*). In short, a relational model for multi-agent epistemic model is a tuple $N = (W, R, V)$ such that (i) W is the domain, (ii) $R : \mathsf{Ag} \to \wp(W \times W)$ assigns every agent a binary relation $R(a)$ on W (which does not need to be an equivalence relation, but just any binary relation will do), and (iii) $V : \mathsf{Prop} \to \wp(W)$ assigns every propositional variable a set of states. The satisfaction of a given formula φ at a state s in N (denoted $N, s \Vdash \varphi$) is defined just as in standard modal logic (cf., e.g., [2]). In particular, $N, s \Vdash K_a \varphi$ iff for all $t \in W$, if $(s, t) \in R(a)$ then $N, t \Vdash \varphi$.

We observe that ELW is reducible to the standard multi-agent epistemic logic over relational models. We show this by the following definition and lemma.

Definition 3.4 We define a translation $\cdot^r$ from weighted models to relational models, such that for a given weighted model $M = (W, A, E, C, \nu)$, M^r is a relational model (W, R, V) with the same domain and:

- R is such that for every $a \in \mathsf{Ag}$, $R(a) = \{(s, t) \in W \mid C(a) \subseteq E(s, t)\}$;
- V is such that for every $p \in \mathsf{Prop}$, $V(p) = \{s \in W \mid p \in \nu(s)\}$.

Lemma 3.5 *For any formula φ, any weighted model M and any state s of M, $M, s \models \varphi$ iff $M^r, s \Vdash \varphi$.*

Proof. By induction on φ. Let $M = (W, A, E, C, \nu)$ be any weighted model and $M^r = (W, R, V)$ its translation. The atomic case is easy by the definition of the translation. Boolean cases follow easily from the definition of satisfaction.

The only interesting case here is that for the K_a operator:

$$\begin{aligned}
M,s \models K_a\psi &\iff \text{for all } t \in W, \text{ if } C(a) \subseteq E(s,t) \text{ then } M,t \models \psi \\
&\iff \text{for all } t \in W, \text{ if } (s,t) \in R(a) \text{ then } M,t \models \psi \\
&\iff \text{for all } t \in W, \text{ if } (s,t) \in R(a) \text{ then } M^r,t \Vdash \psi \quad \text{(IH)} \\
&\iff M^r,s \Vdash K_a\psi.
\end{aligned}$$

The induction step holds, and so we achieve the lemma. $\qquad\square$

Less obviously, we can also reduce the standard multi-agent epistemic logic over relational models to ELW, by playing a tiny trick on the set of abstract abilities.

Definition 3.6 We define a translation $\cdot^w$ from relational models to weighted models, such that for a given relational model $N = (W, R, V)$, N^w is a weighted model $(W, \mathsf{Ag}, E, C, \nu)$ with the same domain and:

- E is such that for all $s, t \in W$, $E(s,t) = \{a \in \mathsf{Ag} \mid (s,t) \in R(a)\}$,
- C is such that for all $a \in \mathsf{Ag}$, $C(a) = \{a\}$, and
- ν is such that for all $s \in W$, $\nu(s) = \{p \in \mathsf{Prop} \mid s \in V(p)\}$.

In the the translated model N^w of the above definition, the collection of epistemic abilities is set to be Ag. We use agents as labels of edges, which can be understood intuitively to be that an agent cannot distinguish the ongoing state from current state, with its epistemic abilities considered as a whole.

In the following lemma, we show that the above defined translation preserves truth.

Lemma 3.7 *For any formula φ, any relational model N and any state s of N, $N, s \Vdash \varphi$ iff $N^w, s \models \varphi$.*

Proof. Let $N = (W, R, V)$ and its translation $N^w = (W, \mathsf{Ag}, E, C, \nu)$. We show the lemma by induction on φ. The atomic and boolean cases are easy to verify. Here we only show the case for the knowledge operator:

$$\begin{aligned}
N,s \Vdash K_a\psi &\iff \text{for all } t \in W, \text{ if } (s,t) \in R(a) \text{ then } N,t \Vdash \psi \\
&\iff \text{for all } t \in W, \text{ if } a \in E(s,t) \text{ then } N,t \Vdash \psi \\
&\iff \text{for all } t \in W, \text{ if } C(a) \subseteq E(s,t) \text{ then } N,t \Vdash \psi \\
&\iff \text{for all } t \in W, \text{ if } C(a) \subseteq E(s,t) \text{ then } N^w,t \models \psi \quad \text{(IH)} \\
&\iff N^w,s \models K_a\psi
\end{aligned}$$

This finishes the proof. $\qquad\square$

Let $\mathbf{K_m}$ be the well-known axiomatization for modal logic (multi-agent version with each K_a a box operator; cf. [2]).

Theorem 3.8 $\mathbf{K_m}$ *is sound and strongly complete with respect to the class of all weighted models. Namely,*

- *(Soundness) for any formula φ, if $\vdash_{\mathbf{K_m}} \varphi$, then φ is valid in ELW;*
- *(Completeness) for any formula φ and any set Φ of formulas, if φ is a logical consequence of Φ in ELW (denoted $\Phi \models_{ELW} \varphi$), then $\Phi \vdash_{\mathbf{K_m}} \varphi$.*

Proof. Soundness. Suppose $\vdash_{\mathbf{K_m}} \varphi$. For any weighted model M and any state s of M, it suffices to show that $M, s \models \varphi$. By the soundness of $\mathbf{K_m}$ over relational models, $M^r, s \Vdash \varphi$. It then follows from Lemma 3.5 that $M, s \models \varphi$, as we wanted to show.

Completeness. Suppose $\Phi \nvdash_{\mathbf{K_m}} \varphi$. By the completeness of $\mathbf{K_m}$ over relational models, there exists a relational model N and a state s of N such that $N, s \Vdash \psi$ for all $\psi \in \Phi$ and $N, s \Vdash \neg\varphi$. By Lemma 3.7, $N^w, s \models \psi$ (for all $\psi \in \Phi$) and $N^w, s \models \neg\varphi$. It follows that $\Phi \nvDash_{ELW} \varphi$.   □

3.3 Computational complexity

In this section we study the complexity of model and validity checking problems for ELW.

As a corollary of Theorem 3.8, whether a formula φ is valid is equivalent to the question of whether it is a theorem of $\mathbf{K_m}$. This is in turn equivalent to the question whether φ is valid in standard multi-agent modal logic $\mathrm{K_m}$, which is known to be PSPACE complete [7]. So we have the following theorem.

Theorem 3.9 *The validity checking problem for ELW is PSPACE complete.*

We then move our focus to the model checking problem for ELW. We first define the measure of input.

Definition 3.10 The *length of a formula* φ, denoted $|\varphi|$, is defined as usual: the length of φ is the number of all the propositional variables and boolean and modal operators that occur in φ.

The *size* of a weighed model $M = (W, A, E, C, \nu)$, denoted $|M|$, with respect to a given formula φ, is the sum of the following:

- $|W|$, i.e., the cardinality of the domain,
- $|A|$, i.e., the cardinality of the set of epistemic abilities,
- $|E|$, defined to be $|W|^2 \cdot |A|$,
- $|C|$ w.r.t. φ, which is defined as $|\varphi| \cdot |A|$, and
- $|\nu|$ w.r.t. φ, defined to be $|W| \cdot |\varphi|$.

Finally, given a weighted model M and formula φ, the *size of the input* is $|M| + |\varphi|$.

Theorem 3.11 *The model checking problem for ELW is in P.*

Proof. Given a weighted model $M = (W, A, E, C, \nu)$, a state $s \in W$ and a formula φ, we need to decide whether $M, s \models \varphi$. In order to do so, we present an algorithm (Algorithm 1) for calculating $Val(M, \varphi)$, the truth set of φ in M, i.e., $\{s \in W \mid M, s \models \varphi\}$. Model checking for $M, s \models \varphi$ is thus reduced to the membership testing in $Val(M, \varphi)$, which takes at most $|W|$ steps in addition to the time costs on computing $Val(M, \varphi)$.

It is not hard to verify that $Val(M, \varphi)$ is indeed the set of states of M at

Algorithm 1 Computing Truthset
___
Require:

        $M = (W, A, E, C, \nu)$ is a weighted model

        φ is a formula

1: **function** $Val(M, \varphi)$

2:     **if** $\varphi = p$ **then return** $\{s \in W \mid p \in \nu(s)\}$

3:     **else if** $\varphi = \neg\psi$ **then return** $W \setminus Val(M, \psi)$

4:     **else if** $\varphi = \psi \to \chi$ **then return** $(W \setminus Val(M, \psi)) \cup Val(M, \chi)$

5:     **else if** $\varphi = K_a\psi$ **then**

6:         **initialize** $tmpVal = \emptyset$

7:         **for all** $t \in W$ **do**

8:            **initialize** $n = true$

9:            **for all** $u \in W$ **do**

10:               **if** $C(a) \subseteq E(t, u)$ **and** $u \notin Val(M, \psi)$ **then** $n \leftarrow false$

11:            **if** $n = true$ **then** $tmpVal \leftarrow tmpVal \cup \{t\}$

12:         **return** $tmpVal$

13:         ▷ *This returns* $\{t \in W \mid \forall u \in W : C(a) \subseteq E(t, u) \Rightarrow u \in Val(M, \psi)\}$
___

which φ is true. In particular, in the case for the K_a operator,

$$
\begin{aligned}
M, s \models K_a\psi \iff& \forall u \in W : C(a) \subseteq E(s, u) \Rightarrow M, u \models \psi \\
\iff& \forall u \in W : C(a) \subseteq E(s, u) \Rightarrow u \in Val(M, \psi) \quad \text{(IH)} \\
\iff& s \in \{t \in W \mid \forall u \in W : C(a) \subseteq E(s, u) \Rightarrow u \in Val(M, \psi)\}
\end{aligned}
$$

The cost for computing $Val(M, \varphi)$ is in polynomial time. In particular, in the case for $K_a\psi$, there are two while-loops over W, and checking $C(a) \subseteq E(t, u)$ costs at most $|A|$ steps, and the membership checking $u \notin Val(M, \psi)$ takes at most $|W|$ steps; this costs $|W|^2 \cdot (|A| + |W|)$. The algorithm for computing $Val(M, \varphi)$ calls itself recursively, but only for a subformula of φ, and the maximum number of recursion is bounded by $|\varphi|$, i.e., the length of φ. So the total time cost for computing $Val(M, \varphi)$ is $|W|^2 \cdot (|A| + |W|) \cdot |\varphi|$.

Considering the input size, we find that the total time cost is within $O(n^2)$. So the theorem holds. ☐

4   Epistemic Logic over Similarity Models (ELS)

In this section we study epistemic logic over similarity models (ELS for short). That is, the formulas are interpreted with weighted models in which the binary relations between states stand for the similarity relations.

Let $\mathbf{KB_m}$ be the axiomatization achieved by adding an extra axiom B (i.e., $\varphi \to K_a\neg K_a\neg\varphi$) to $\mathbf{K_m}$, which is known to be a sound and strongly complete axiomatization for the standard epistemic logic interpreted with the class of all relational models in which the binary relation is symmetric (henceforth called *symmetric relational models*). We now show that $\mathbf{KB_m}$ is also a sound and strongly complete axiomatization for ELS.

Lemma 4.1 *The following results hold for the translations:*

(i) *Given a similarity model M, the translation M^r (see Definition 3.4) is a symmetric relational model;*

(ii) *Given a symmetric relational model N, the translation N^w (see Definition 3.6) is a weighted model satisfying symmetry (cf. Definition 2.2).*

Proof. (i) Let $M = (W, A, E, C, \nu)$ be a similarity model, and its translation $M^r = (W, R, V)$. For any $a \in \mathsf{Ag}$ and $s, t \in W$, we have:

$$
\begin{aligned}
(s, t) \in R(a) &\iff C(a) \subseteq E(s, t) \text{ (Def. 3.4)} \\
&\iff C(a) \subseteq E(t, s) \text{ (by symmetry, see Def. 2.2)} \\
&\iff (t, s) \in R(a). \quad \text{(Def. 3.4)}
\end{aligned}
$$

Thus M^r is a symmetric relational model.

(ii) Let $N = (W, R, V)$ be a symmetric relational model, and its translation $N^w = (W, \mathsf{Ag}, E, C, \nu)$. For any $a \in \mathsf{Ag}$ and $s, t \in W$, we have:

$$
\begin{aligned}
a \in E(s, t) &\iff (s, t) \in R(a) \text{ (Def. 3.6)} \\
&\iff (t, s) \in R(a) \text{ (since } R \text{ is symmetric)} \\
&\iff a \in E(t, s). \quad \text{(Def. 3.6)}
\end{aligned}
$$

Hence N^w is a weighted model satisfying symmetry.   □

Theorem 4.2 $\mathbf{KB_m}$ *is sound and strongly complete with respect to the class of all similarity models. Namely,*

- *(Soundness) for any formula φ, if $\vdash_{\mathbf{KB_m}} \varphi$, then φ is valid in ELS;*
- *(Completeness) for any formula φ and any set Φ of formulas, if φ is a logical consequence of Φ in ELS (denoted $\Phi \models_{ELS} \varphi$), then $\Phi \vdash_{\mathbf{KB_m}} \varphi$.*

Proof. Soundness. Given a formula φ, a similarity model M and a state s of M, suppose $\vdash_{\mathbf{KB_m}} \varphi$. It follows from Lemma 4.1(i) that M^r is a symmetric relational model. By the soundness of $\mathbf{KB_m}$ over symmetric relational models, we have $M^r, s \Vdash \varphi$. By Lemma 3.5, we have $M, s \models \varphi$.

Completeness. For a formula φ and a set Φ of formulas, suppose $\Phi \nvdash_{\mathbf{KB_m}} \varphi$. By the completeness of $\mathbf{KB_m}$ over symmetric relational models, we have a symmetric relational model N and a state s of it such that $N, s \Vdash \psi$ (for all $\psi \in \Phi$) and $N, s \Vdash \neg\varphi$. By Lemmas 4.1(ii) and 3.7, the translation model N^w is a symmetric weighted model and $N^w, s \models \psi$ (for all $\psi \in \Phi$) and $N^w, s \models \neg\varphi$.

Suppose $N^w = (W, A, E, C, \nu)$, and define $M = (W, A \cup \{b\}, E, C, \nu)$ with b a new epistemic ability (i.e., $b \notin A$). M is a similarity model, since positivity holds as there cannot be any $s, t \in W$ such that $E(s, t) = A \cup \{b\}$ and $s \neq t$. Moreover, we can show that for any formula χ, $N^w, s \models \chi$ iff $M, s \models \chi$. Therefore, $\Phi \nvDash_{ELS} \varphi$.   □

From the proof of Theorem 4.2, we also get the following.

Corollary 4.3 $\mathbf{KB_m}$ *is sound and strongly complete with respect to the class of all symmetric weighted models.*

Finally we introduce the computational complexity results for ELS.

Theorem 4.4 (i) *The validity problem for ELS is PSPACE complete.*
(ii) *The model checking problem for ELS is in P.*

Proof. (i) By Theorem 4.2, whether a formula φ is valid in ELS is equivalent
to the question of whether it is a theorem of $\mathbf{KB_m}$. This is in turn equivalent
to the question whether φ is valid in standard multimodal logic $\mathrm{KB_m}$, which is
known to be PSPACE hard [3] (in fact it is shown there that the unimodal logic
KB is PSPACE complete). The PSPACE upper bound can be shown using a
similar method to that presented in [7] for the multimodal logic $\mathrm{K_m}$. We leave
a detailed proof in a technical appendix.

(ii) The model checking problem for ELS is a subproblem of that for ELW.
While the latter is in P (Theorem 3.11), so is the former. $\square$

5 Conclusion

We introduced epistemic logics over weighted models and similarity models,
showed by reductions that the axiomatizations $\mathbf{K_m}$ and $\mathbf{KB_m}$ are sound and
complete for them respectively, and identified the computation complexity results for the model and validity checking problems for these logics. For future
work we are interested in more sophisticated conditions on the similarity relation, such as introduced in [4]. It is also useful to compare our framework with
existing ones, such as those presented in [12,5].

References

[1] Aggarwal, C. C., "Data Mining: The Textbook," Springer, 2015.
[2] Blackburn, P., M. De Rijke and Y. Venema, "Modal logic," Cambridge Tracts in
   Theoretical Computer Science **53**, Cambridge University Press, 2001.
[3] Chen, C.-C. and I.-P. Lin, *The computational complexity of the satisfiability of modal
   Horn clauses for modal propositional logics*, Theoretical Computer Science **129** (1994),
   pp. 95–121.
[4] Chen, S., B. Ma and K. Zhang, *On the similarity metric and the distance metric*,
   Theoretical Computer Science **410** (2009), pp. 2365–2376.
[5] Dong, H., X. Li and Y. N. Wáng, *Weighted modal logic in epistemic and deontic contexts*,
   in: S. Ghosh and T. Icard, editors, *Proceedings of the Eighth International Conference on
   Logic, Rationality and Interaction (LORI 2021)*, Lecture Notes of Theoretical Computer
   Science **13039** (2021), pp. 73–87.
[6] Fagin, R., J. Y. Halpern, Y. Moses and M. Y. Vardi, "Reasoning about knowledge," The
   MIT Press, 1995.
[7] Halpern, J. Y. and Y. Moses, *A guide to completeness and complexity for modal logics
   of knowledge and belief*, Artificial Intelligence **54** (1992), pp. 319–379.
[8] Hansen, M., K. G. Larsen, R. Mardare and M. R. Pedersen, *Reasoning about bounds in
   weighted transition systems*, LMCS **14** (2018), pp. 1–32.
[9] Hintikka, J., "Knowledge and Belief: An Introduction to the Logic of Two Notions,"
   Cornell University Press, Ithaca, New York, 1962.
[10] Larsen, K. G. and R. Mardare, *Complete proof systems for weighted modal logic*,
   Theoretical Computer Science **546** (2014), pp. 164–175.
[11] Meyer, J.-J. C. and W. van der Hoek, "Epistemic Logic for AI and Computer Science,"
   Cambridge University Press, 1995.
[12] Naumov, P. and J. Tao, *Logic of confidence*, Synthese **192** (2015), pp. 1821–1838.
[13] Tan, P.-N., M. Steinbach and V. Kumar, "Introduction to data mining," Pearson, 2005.

A   Appendix

We fill in the gap in Theorem 4.4(i), namely, we prove the PSPACE upper bound of the validity problem for ELS. The method is adapted from [7] where tableaux are introduced to show the PSPACE upper bound of the validity problem for the multimodal logic K_m.

Recall that Ag is the (finite) set of agents we are concerned with, and here we are working with the classical multi-modal language (where for each $a \in \mathsf{Ag}$, the operator K_a is a standard modal box operator).

We first introduce the notions of *tableaux* (Definitions A.1–A.3), and then show that a formula φ is KB_m satisfiable if and only if there is an open tableau for φ (Lemma A.4). Then we introduce an algorithm (Algorithm 3) for computing whether there is an open tableau extending a given pre-tableau. This gives us a decision procedure for the KB_m satisfiability problem (also by Lemma A.4) and we show that the decision procedure is bounded in polynomial space (Theorem A.6).

Definition A.1 A *pre-tableau* is a pair (W, R, L), where:

- W is a nonempty set of states;
- $R : \mathsf{Ag} \to \wp(W \times W)$ is a function maping every agent to a binary relation on W;
- L is a function mapping every state to a set of formulas.

Definition A.2 A triple (W, R, L) is called an *open tableau*, if is a pre-tableau such that for any $s, t \in W$, $a \in Ag$ and any formulas φ and ψ:

 (i) If $(s, t) \in R(a)$, then $(t, s) \in R(a)$;

 (ii) If $\neg\neg\varphi \in L(s)$, then $\varphi \in L(s)$;

 (iii) If $(\varphi \to \psi) \in L(s)$, then $\neg\varphi \in L(s)$ or $\psi \in L(s)$;

 (iv) If $\neg(\varphi \to \psi) \in L(s)$, then $\varphi \in L(s)$ and $\neg\psi \in L(s)$;

 (v) If $K_a\varphi \in L(s)$ and $(s, t) \in R(a)$, then $\varphi \in L(t)$;

 (vi) If $\neg K_a\varphi \in L(s)$, then there exists $t \in W$ such that $(s, t) \in R(a)$ and $\neg\varphi \in L(t)$;

(vii) It is not the case that both φ and $\neg\varphi$ are in $L(s)$.

Definition A.3 Let φ be a formula, an *open tableau for* φ is a tuple (W, R, L, s), where (W, R, L) forms an open tableau, $s \in W$ and $\varphi \in L(s)$.

Now we show that an open tableau for a formula actually witnesses the satisfiability of the formula.

Lemma A.4 *Let φ be a formula. There exists an open tableau for φ, if and only if, φ is KB_m satisfiable.*

Proof. From left to right. Let (W, R, L, s) be an open tableau for φ. Let $M = (W, R, V)$ be a relational model, such that for every $p \in \mathsf{Prop}$, $V(p) = \{s \in W \mid p \in L(s)\}$. It is not hard to verify that M is a symmetric relational model.

Now we prove that for any $t \in W$ and any formula ψ,

- $\psi \in L(t)$ implies $M, t \Vdash \psi$, and
- $\neg\psi \in L(t)$ implies $M, t \Vdash \neg\psi$.

We show it by induction on ψ. The atomic and boolean cases are easy to verify by the definition of M and definition A.2. Here we only show the case for the modal operator:

$$K_a\psi \in L(t) \implies \text{for all } t' \in W, \text{ if } (t, t') \in R(a) \text{ then } \psi \in L(t')$$
$$\implies \text{for all } t' \in W, \text{ if } (t, t') \in R(a) \text{ then } M, t' \Vdash \psi \text{ (IH)}$$
$$\implies M, t \Vdash K_a\psi$$

$$\neg K_a\psi \in L(t) \implies \text{there is } t' \in W \text{ s.t. } (t, t') \in R(a) \text{ and } \neg\psi \in L(t')$$
$$\implies \text{there is } t' \in W \text{ s.t. } (t, t') \in R(a) \text{ and } M, t' \Vdash \neg\psi \text{ (IH)}$$
$$\implies M, t \Vdash \neg K_a\psi.$$

From right to left. Suppose φ is $\mathrm{KB_m}$ satisfiable. Then there is a symmetric relational model $M = (W, R, V)$ and a states $s \in W$ such that $M, s \Vdash \varphi$. Let (W, R, L, s) be a pre-tableau such that for every $t \in W$, $L(t) = \{\chi \mid M, t \Vdash \chi\}$. It is not hard to verify that (W, R, L, s) satisfies Definitions A.2 and A.3, hence is an open tableau for φ. $\square$

Next we introduce an algorithm for deciding whether a pre-tableau is extendable to an open tableau, in the sense that it tells us whether for a given pre-tableau (W, R, L), there is an open tableau (W', R', L') such that $W \subseteq W'$, $R \subseteq R'$ and for every $s \in W$, $L(s) \subseteq L'(s)$. The algorithm is presented in Algorithms 2 and 3, where a function $Open$ is introduced to determine whether a pre-tableau is extendable to an open tableau. By applying the above lemma (Lemma A.4), the algorithm will play an essential role in deciding whether a formula is $\mathrm{KB_m}$ satisfiable.

Algorithm 2 Generating witnessing states for modal diamonds

Require:
        (W, R, L) is a pre-tableau
        $s \in W$
        $u \notin W$
        $\varphi = \neg K_a\psi$ where $a \in \mathsf{Ag}$ and ψ is a formula

1: **function** $Grow(W, R, L, s, \varphi)$
2:     **for all** $t \in W$ **do**
3:         **if** $(s, t) \in R(a)$ **and** $\neg\psi \in L(t)$ **then return false**
4:     $W \leftarrow W \cup \{u\}$
5:     $R(a) \leftarrow R(a) \cup \{(s, u)\}$
6:     $L(u) \leftarrow \{\neg\psi\} \cup \{\chi \mid K_a\chi \in L(s)\}$
7:     **return** W, R, L

Lemma A.5 *For any pre-tableau (W, R, L), (i) if $Open(W, R, L)$ returns **true** then the pre-tableau is extendable to an open tableau, and (ii) if $Open(W, R, L)$ returns **false** then the pre-tableau is not extendable to an open tableau.*

Algorithm 3 Deciding whether a pre-tableau is extendable to an open tableau

---

Require: (W, R, L) is a pre-tableau
1: **function** $Open(W, R, L)$
2:     **for all** $s \in W$ **do**
3:         **for all** $a \in \text{Ag}$ **do**
4:             **if** $(s, t) \in R(a)$ **and** $(t, s) \notin R(a)$ **then**
5:                 $R(a) \leftarrow R(a) \cup \{(t, s)\}$
6:                 **return** $Open(W, R, L)$
7:     **for all** $s \in W$ **do**
8:         **for all** $\varphi \in L(s)$ **do**
9:             **if** $\varphi = \neg\neg\psi$ **and** $\psi \notin L(s)$ **then**
10:                 $L(s) \leftarrow L(s) \cup \{\psi\}$
11:                 **return** $Open(W, R, L)$
12:             **else if** $\varphi = (\psi \to \chi)$ **and** $\neg\psi \notin L(s)$ **and** $\chi \notin L(s)$ **then**
13:                 $L' \leftarrow L$
14:                 $L'' \leftarrow L$
15:                 $L'(s) \leftarrow L'(s) \cup \{\neg\psi\}$
16:                 $L''(s) \leftarrow L''(s) \cup \{\chi\}$
17:                 **if** $Open(W, R, L') = $ **true or** $Open(W, R, L'') = $ **true then**
18:                     **return true**
19:                 **else**
20:                     **return false**
21:             **else if** $\varphi = \neg(\psi \to \chi)$ **and** $[\psi \notin L(s)$ **or** $\neg\chi \notin L(s)]$ **then**
22:                 $L(s) \leftarrow L(s) \cup \{\psi, \neg\chi\}$
23:                 **return** $Open(W, R, L)$
24:     **for all** $s \in W$ **do**
25:         **for all** $t \in W$ **do**
26:             **for all** $a \in \text{Ag}$ **do**
27:                 **for all** $\varphi \in L(s)$ **do**
28:                     **if** $\varphi = K_a\psi$ **and** $(s, t) \in R(a)$ **and** $\psi \notin L(t)$ **then**
29:                       $L(t) \leftarrow L(t) \cup \{\psi\}$
30:                       **return** $Open(W, R, L)$
31:     **for all** $s \in W$ **do**
32:         **for all** $a \in \text{Ag}$ **do**
33:             **for all** $\varphi \in L(s)$ **do**
34:                 **if** $\varphi = \neg K_a\psi$ **then**
35:                   **if** $Grow(W, R, L, s, \varphi) = $ **false then continue**
36:                   **return** $Open(Grow(W, R, L, s, \varphi))$
37:     **for all** $s \in W$ **do**
38:         **for all** $\varphi \in L(s)$ **do**
39:             **if** $\neg\varphi \in L(s)$ **then**
40:                 **return false**
41:     **return true**

Proof. Let (W, R, L) be a pre-tableau. We prove the lemma by induction on the number n of recursive calls of Algorithm 3 itself (where the function $Grow$ is presented in Algorithm 2).

Basic step. If $n = 0$, then the algorithm does not recursively call itself. So the input pre-tableau (W, R, L) does not update during the process. In this case, either (W, R, L) satisfies all the conditions in Definition A.2, making itself an open tableau (so the process will pass through the loops and return **true** by the last line), or it reaches Line 36 of Algorithm 3 and returns **false** in the loop (in this case there are φ and $\neg\varphi$ in $L(s)$ so that there are no open tableau extending (W, R, V)). The lemma holds in both cases.

Inductive step. Suppose the lemma holds whenever $Open(W, R, L)$ recursively calls itself less than k times. Suppose now $Open(W, R, L)$ recursively calls itself k times. It suffices to show that the lemma holds as well.

Case (i). The kth recursive call returns **true**. There must be a pre-tableau (W', R', L') such that $Open(W', R', L')$ is called during the recursive processes and it returns **true**. (For the case of implication, it generate two subcases, but at least one of them returns **true**.) By the induction hypothesis, (W', R', L') is extendable to an open tableau, so is (W, R, L) since (W', R', L') extends (W, R, L).

Case (ii). The kth recursive call returns **false**. Then all the recursive calls return **false** (in particular, the reader can verify the case for implication). By the induction hypothesis, for all $Open(W', R', L')$ executed during the recursive process, (W', R', L') must not be extendable to an open tableau. Since every (W', R', L') extends (W, R, L), we have that (W, R, L) is also not extendable to an open tableau. Suppose towards a contradiction that this is not case, i.e., (W, R, L) is extendable to an open tableau. Then we extend it to a minimal open tableau (i.e., a minimal one satisfying all the conditions in Lemma A.2). Since Algothrim 3 truthfully implements these conditions, such an open tableau must be one of the (W', R', L') mentioned above, which contradicts with that (W', R', L') is not extendable to an open tableau. $\square$

Theorem A.6 *The validity problem for KB_m is in PSPACE.*

Proof. To prove that the validity problem of KB_m is in PSPACE, it is sufficient to show that the satisfiability problem of KB_m is in co-PSPACE. Since it is known that co-PSPACE = PSPACE, it is sufficient to give an PSPACE algorithm for testing whether a given formula is KB_m satisfiable.

For a given formula φ, first define a pre-tableau (W, R, L) such that $W = \{s\}$, $R = \emptyset$ and $L(s) = \{\varphi\}$. Then we execute $Open(W, R, L)$ provided in Algorithm 3. Because $L(s)$ is a set of a single formula, during the process of recursively calling the algorithm, only its subformulas and their negations can appear in extended pre-tableaux, so the process always halts. By Lemma A.5, the output of Algorithm 3 is **true**, if and only if, there exists an open tableau for φ, which is equivalent to the fact that φ is KB_m satisfiable by Lemma A.4.

We complete the proof by showing that $Open(W, R, L)$ terminates in PSPACE in size of the input. As usual, the size of the input φ is counted as $|\varphi|$, i.e., the length of φ. The size of the pre-tableau (W, R, L) given above is $|\varphi| + c$ for some constant natural number c.

Since in the process, new states are introduced only when moving from a formula to one of its subformulas (or its negation), so there will be at most $2 \cdot |\varphi|$ states. For a similar reason, for any state u appeared in the process, there are at most $2 \cdot |\varphi|$ formulas in $L(u)$. So the size of expanded pre-tableau (in particular, the finally generated open tableau) is bounded by $2 \cdot |\varphi| + (2 \cdot |\varphi|)^2 + (2 \cdot |\varphi|) \cdot (2 \cdot |\varphi|)$. So the space cost is polynomial.

The above gives us a PSPACE algorithm for deciding whether a given formula is KB_m satisfiable. $\qquad\qquad\square$

Decision Making with Weighted Quantitative Argumentation Based on Regression

Puyin Li [1], Dov Gabbay [2]

ZLAIRE, Zhejiang University, China
King's College London, United Kingdom
University of Luxembourg, Luxembourg

Xiao Chi [3], You Cheng [4]

University College London, United Kingdom
ZLAIRE, Zhejiang University, China

Abstract

In this paper we introduce a weighted quantitative argumentation framework based on regression, which is an extension of Baroni et al.'s quantitative argumentation framework. Our model implements the method of regression to assign base scores to arguments and method of cosine distance to assign weights to the attack or support relations between arguments. In practice, the model aligns a decision-making process where both real-time information and decisions made based on historical information are considered, and finds a way to make a decision taking account of both current and historical knowledge. A typical application area is selling and buying houses where people refer to both historical and real-time information.

Keywords: Argumentation, Weighted Argumentation, QuAD, Regression.

1 Introduction

Data sets and regression models based on them have been implemented wide and far in various subjects and areas in the past two centuries. When making decisions about a case or a problem, people have an increasing tendency to refer to large databases which describe various aspects of the cases. Hence, data science has prospered during the past century. Nevertheless, despite the boost of data science and mathematical logic these days, discussions are still rare on how human-level knowledge (bargaining, reasoning, negotiation, etc.) can be related, expressed, and presented in data sets that contain numerous empirical

---

[1] puyin.li@zju.edu.cn

[2] dov.gabbay@kcl.ac.uk

[3] cx3506@outlook.com

[4] ichyou@zju.edu.cn

information. One typical case of how human-level knowledge is involved with objective data analysis is how people refer to past decisions to make a decision in the future. Our work aims at extracting and presenting human-level knowledge in the decision making process where both data at the present, data in the past, and decisions made in the past makes a difference. This goal is achieved by implementing logic as well as mathematical tools such as formal argumentation and regression.

Our model is suitable for dealing with a setting where information is provided as follows (think of buying and selling houses):

- A data set presenting the information needed for a decision being made where regression can be applied to help the decision;

- Historical data sets as references for decisions made in the past;

- Present user's preferences and past users' preferences.

Given the above information, we design a regression-based quantitative argumentation model which helps to make decisions under such settings.

The paper is organized as follows. Section 2 provides background on both regression and argumentation frameworks, and specifies a sample case of recommending a house property to a potential customer. Following that, Section 3 introduces the idea of a weighted quantitative argumentation framework based on regression with definitions and detailed discussion using the house or flat purchasing case as a typical example. It also demonstrates how recommending scores can be calculated and how explanations are generated by the argumentation framework. Then, Section 4 is a comparison of our work with other related papers. The last section draws a conclusion on what we have achieved so far, specifies some limitations of the work, and points out some future work that may be carried out based on what we have done.

2   Background

2.1   Abstract quantitative argumentation frameworks

We first introduce the idea of formal argumentation [3] used in this paper. As introduced by Dung [11], core concepts of abstract formal argumentation include argumentation frameworks and some basic semantics for the frameworks.

Definition 2.1 An argumentation framework is a tuple $AF = \langle A, R \rangle$, where A is a set of arguments and $R \subseteq A \times A$ is a set of attacks.

According to this definition, for two arguments α, β in AF , we use $(\alpha, \beta) \in R$ to denote that α attacks β. And with the attack relation between arguments, we can further define relation between sets of arguments and single arguments, as well as the properties of such sets.

Definition 2.2 Let $AF = \langle A, R \rangle$ be an argumentation framework.

- A set $S \subseteq A$ of arguments is *conflict-free* if and only if there is no $\alpha, \beta \in S$ such that $(\alpha, \beta) \in R$.

- An argument $\alpha \in A$ is *acceptable* with regard to a set $S \subseteq A$, if and only if $\forall (\beta, \alpha) \in R$, $\exists \gamma \in S$ such that $(\gamma, \beta) \in R$.

- A conflict-free set of arguments $S \subseteq A$ is admissible if and only if each argument in S is acceptable with regard to S.

Having the notions of acceptable arguments and admissible sets in place, we can have different types of extensions(admissible sets): a *preferred extension* of AF is a maximal (with regard to set inclusion) admissible set of AF; a *stable extension* of AF is a conflict-free set of arguments that attacks each argument in A which does not belong to itself; a *complete extension* of AF is an admissible set of arguments which contains every argument in A that is acceptable with regard to itself; and a *grounded extension* of AF is the minimal (with regard to set inclusion) complete extension of AF.

This argumentation framework initially created by Dung is restrictive in the following two aspects: first, it only discusses attack relations and leaves out support relations; and second, the acceptability of arguments are binary - an argument can only be either accepted or not accepted. But in real scenarios of reasoning, the relations between arguments can be more sophisticated, and the status of arguments are less determined than either to be accepted or not. Therefore, bipolar argumentation frameworks with attack and support relations [6,2,15] and quantitative argumentation frameworks where arguments also have strength [4,18] are developed on the basis of Dung's initial abstract argumentation.

Definition 2.3 An abstract bipolar argumentation framework is a triple $\mathcal{A} = \langle \mathcal{A}, \mathcal{R}^+, \mathcal{R}^- \rangle$, where $\mathcal{A}$ is a set of arguments, $\mathcal{R}^+ \subseteq \mathcal{A} \times \mathcal{A}$ is a set of support relations and $\mathcal{R}^- \subseteq \mathcal{A} \times \mathcal{A}$ is a set of attack relations.

Definition 2.4 Let $\mathcal{AF} = \langle \mathcal{A}, \mathcal{R}^+, \mathcal{R}^- \rangle$ be a bipolar argumentation framework, $A_1, A_n, B \in \mathcal{A}$, and $R_i \in \mathcal{R}^+ \cup \mathcal{R}^-$.

- A *supported attack* for an argument B is a sequence $A_1 R_1 ... R_{n-1} A_n, n \geq 3$, with $A_n = B$, such that $\forall i = 2, ..., n-2, R_i \in \mathcal{R}^+$ and $R_{n-1} \in \mathcal{R}^-$.

To give numerical representations of the strengths of arguments, quantitative argumentation framework is developed on top of the bipolar argumentation framework. Here we present simpler and more concentrated version of Baroni's QuAD framework [4].

Definition 2.5 An quantitative argumentation framework is a 4-tuple $\mathcal{AF} = \langle \mathcal{A}, \mathcal{R}^+, \mathcal{R}^-, \mathcal{BS} \rangle$, such that for the scale $\mathbb{I} \in [-1, 1]$, $\mathcal{A}$ is a set of arguments, $\mathcal{R}^+$ is a set of support relations, $\mathcal{R}^-$ is a set of attack relations, and $\mathcal{BS} : \mathcal{A} \to \mathbb{I}$ is a total function denoting argument a's base score as $\mathcal{BS}(a)$.

With base scores added to the bipolar argumentation framework, we can assign a generic score to arguments in the argumentation framework according to the structure of the argumentation framework and the base scores of arguments.

Definition 2.6 A *generic score function* for an argument a in a quantitative argumentation framework is $\mathcal{SF} = g(\mathcal{BS}(a), \mathcal{F}_{att}(\mathcal{BS}(a), SEQ_{\mathcal{SF}}(\mathcal{R}^-(a))), \mathcal{F}_{supp}(\mathcal{BS}(a), SEQ_{\mathcal{SF}}(\mathcal{R}^+(a)))$ such that:

- g is a aggregation function such that $g(v_0, v_a, v_s) = $
$$\begin{cases} v_a \ if \ v_s = nil \ and \ v_a \neq nil \\ v_s \ if \ v_s \neq nil \ and \ v_a = nil \\ v_0 \ if \ v_a = v_s = nil \\ \frac{(v_a + v_s)}{2} \ otherwise \end{cases} \; ;$$

- $SEQ_{\mathcal{SF}}$ is a corresponding sequence of attackers or supporters;

- and $\mathcal{F}_{att}, \mathcal{F}_{supp}$ are two functions that return specific values given an argument, a sequence, and the type of relation between the argument and the sequence.

The existing quantitative argumentation models, however, only incorporates the numerical features of the arguments into their calculation. But in practice, we may not only consider how strong each argument is, but also how close each argument is related to other arguments in order to decide whether this argument is strong enough to be accepted. The importance of checking the strength of support or attacks is addressed by some discussions in papers on weighted argumentation frameworks [1,7,8,20], yet existing weighted argumentation frameworks or graphs either only consider weights on individual arguments, or only consider weights on attack/support relations. Publications taking both aspects into account are scarce. Therefore, a viable way of developing the existing quantitative argumentation frameworks [1,7,8,20] is to take both weights on the arguments and weights on the relations into account in the calculation of generic scores. In the next section, we will define what an argument is (in terms of data sets and preferences) and we will discuss how to add weights to attack and support relations to enhance the existing quantitative argumentation frameworks. But before that, we need to have the idea of regression, which gives base scores to the arguments later, and the idea of cosine distance, which characterizes the similarity between two arguments and gives weights to the attack or support relations.

2.2 Regression and cosine distance

Regression models [10,21] the relationship between a dependent variable y and several explanatory variables x_i by fitting an equation to observed data. Usually, the model is decided by the the methods know as *Ordinary Least Squares*. There are different types of regression models such as linear regression, polynomial regression, stepwise regression, etc. But the basic idea is the same: to fit a set of data into a mathematical model, and give estimations and evaluations to certain values in the data set. For every regression model, there are always dependent and independent variables, and an error term representing the difference between the model's estimation and the actual value of the dependent

price	halls	area	floor	subway	school	bedrooms
6.06027	1	55.01044	13	1	0	2
4.920575	2	109.3877	2	0	0	2
3.769788	1	79.69252	11	1	0	2
8.319766	1	52.47666	12	1	1	2
8.077537	1	50.81697	1	1	1	1

Fig. 1. 668-1

variable. To illustrate the idea of regression, we present here first the idea of data sets, and then a simplest and most implemented type, linear regression. For other types, we invite our readers to refer to some more professional books in statistics.

Definition 2.7 A data set is a collection of data. In this paper we present it in the form of a $m \times n$ matrix, where every column of a table corresponds to a variable/attribute, and every row corresponds to a record/item.

Example 2.8 The graph above, for example, presents a 5×7 data set, where each row represents the information about a house and each column represents an attribute. Among all the attributes here, the attribute "price" is dependent on others, and can be regarded as a dependent variable in regression models.

Definition 2.9 Given a data set $\{y_i, x_{i1}, x_{i2}, ..., x_{ip}\}_{i=1}^n$ of n items, a linear regression model assumes that the relationship between the dependent variable y and the p-vector regressors $\mathbf{x}$ is linear and takes the form:

$$y_i = \beta_0 + \beta_1 x_{i1} + ... + \beta_p x_{ip} + \varepsilon_i, i = 1, ..., n,$$

where $\beta_0, \beta_1, ..., \beta_p$ are regression coefficients and ε_i is the *error term* (an unobserved random variable that adds "noise" to the regression relationship). Put in the form of matrices, linear regression models can also be denoted more con-

cisely as $: \mathbf{y} = \mathbf{X}\beta + \varepsilon$, where $\mathbf{y} = \begin{pmatrix} y_1 \\ y_2 \\ \vdots \\ y_n \end{pmatrix}$, $\mathbf{X} = \begin{pmatrix} x_1^T \\ x_2^T \\ \vdots \\ x_n^T \end{pmatrix} = \begin{pmatrix} 1 & x_{11} & ... & x_{1p} \\ 1 & x_{21} & ... & x_{2p} \\ \vdots & \vdots & \ddots & \vdots \\ 1 & x_{n1} & ... & x_{np} \end{pmatrix}$,

$\beta = \begin{pmatrix} \beta_0 \\ \beta_1 \\ \vdots \\ \beta_p \end{pmatrix}$, $\varepsilon = \begin{pmatrix} \varepsilon_1 \\ \varepsilon_2 \\ \vdots \\ \varepsilon_n \end{pmatrix}$.

It usually requires a large volume of data and a wise selection of variables to make regression models representative. In the data set presented above, we can add more records to the data set, and then do regression using the price as the dependent variable y, and halls as independent variables $x_1, \ldots, x_n$.

The regression method represents the relationship between one question item and other referential items in a data set. However , to address the nature of the decision-making process based on the data sets more precisely, we also need to consider decisions made in the past and the similarity between the current problem and the past problem. This similarity in the problem is represented by the cosine similarity of the agents' preferences.

Definition 2.10 The cosine similarity [19] between two vectors A and B is
$$S_{A-B} = \frac{AB}{|A||B|} = \frac{\Sigma r_{a,i} r_{b,i}}{\sqrt{\Sigma r_{a,i}^2} \sqrt{\Sigma r_{b,i}^2}} \ .$$

Here, each element $r_{a,i}$ or $r_{b,i}$ in the vectors A or B is a normalized value of the agents preference on one attribute, whether the attribute is numerical, ordinal, or binary.

2.3   Case study: bargaining in buying a house

As we have put it in the introduction part, our model serves to make a decision when (I) data set that characterizes the present situation when the decision in question is made; (II) data sets that characterize historical situations when decisions were made by other agents; and (III) preferences of the current decision-maker and previous decisions makers are provided. A typical scenario that matches this setting is when a real estate agent is trying to recommend housing properties to a potential customer.

If a person is to purchase a house, he may argue with the agent from several aspects. First, whether the house is price worthy compared with other houses at the market at the same time. Second, whether the house caters to his particular preferences and needs. Third, whether the price of the house is plausible compared to previous deals. For example, the purchasing history of a customer's friend tends to influence the buyer's decision significantly. When these three aspects are all well taken care of, the likelihood of a successful recommendation should be high.

The model introduced in the next section incorporates all three aspects in this example and other similar cases where present and historical data, as well as personal preferences, make a difference to the decision. To represent how the present market situation influences the buyer's decisions, we use regression. And to characterize how his preferences and needs influence the decision, we define functions that describe how similar they are with other users and incorporate the functions into a quantitative argumentation framework that eventually gives solutions to the decision.

3 Weighted Quantitative Argumentation Frameworks Based on Regression

In this section, we set up the argumentation framework that helps to make decisions in the setting we have discussed above. We first define what an argument is in a data-based setting like this. Then we construct several indexes that are useful in generating the weighted quantitative argumentation framework. With these elements in place, we can set up the framework and see how to make decisions with it.

3.1 Data-preference-based arguments

To generate an argumentation framework for the above setting, the first step is to clarify what an argument is in such cases. In natural language, a data-preference-based argument comes in the following form: *given the current situation represented by the data set D and the agent's preferences $p_1, p_2, ..., p_n$, the agent should be satisfied with item i.* More specifically, in the house recommendation case, a data-preference-based argument can be put down as follows: *given the housing prices in the market represented by the existing data and the potential customer's preference in transportation, location and facilities, etc., House 1 should be a satisfactory choice for the buyer.*

We can also put this down in formal language as below:

Definition 3.1 A *data-preference based argument* is a tuple $\mathcal{A} = \langle \mathcal{D}, \mathcal{P}, \mathcal{T} \rangle$, where

- $\mathcal{D}$ is a data set with rows representing items and columns representing attributes of these items;

- $\mathcal{P} = \{p_1, p_2, ..., p_n\}$ is a set of agent's preferences, $p_1, ..., p_n$ being independent restrictions on values of the variables in $\mathcal{D}$;

- $\mathcal{T}$ is the target item to be judged and measured.

Example 3.2 Suppose a customer is going to purchase a house in March 2022, and the housing agent has a 10000×100 data set (in the form as presented by Example 2.7) that incorporates information about all the houses on sale in March. Then the customer gives his preferences on the house she wants to buy: (I) it is in Xihu District, Hangzhou, China; (II) it is within 2km from the nearest subway station; (III) it is a school district housing; (IV) It is no more expensive than ¥7,000,000... With these preferences, the buyer or the housing agent can pick out houses that satisfy or nearly satisfy the customer's requirements, which, for example, constitutes a smaller set of 1000×100, and build a regression model to estimate the price of the houses on the market. They may eventually pick out several houses that are available at the moment to decide which one to buy or to recommend to the customer. For each of the houses picked in the data set by the preferences and other considerations, we regard it as an argument.

Data-preference-based arguments defined above tell us information about the relations between a single target house and all other houses on the market at the time when the decision-maker is making the decision. But when making a decision, people also refer to how other people who are similar to them have made their decision in history. The similarity between the decision-maker and past decision-makers is characterized by the cosine similarity between their preferences as defined below.

Definition 3.3 The cosine similarity $S_{\mathcal{P}_i-\mathcal{P}_j}$ between two preference sets $\mathcal{P}_i, \mathcal{P}_j$ is derived through three steps:

- normalize every variable (continuous/discrete/binary/categorical) in $\mathcal{D}$;

- get the normalized values of $p_{i1}, \ldots, p_{in}$ in $\mathcal{P}_i$ and $p_{j1}, \ldots, p_{jn}$ in $\mathcal{P}_j$, denoting as $v_{i1}, \ldots, v_{im}$ and $v_{j1}, \ldots, v_{jm}$;

- the cosine similarity between $\mathcal{P}_i$ and $\mathcal{P}_j$ is then just the cosine similarity between vectors $(v_{i1}, \ldots, v_{im})$ and $(v_{j1}, \ldots, v_{jm})$.

Note that when we are doing the normalization, we may have to break down one variable into two or more dimensions. For example, some categorical variables may be divided into several binary values, and preferences given in the form of intervals may be divided into two values (lower bound and upper bound). Therefore, the dimension of the normalized vectors in the above definition may be higher than the number of rows in the data set.

3.2   Index Construction

Having defined what an argument is in setting when both data and preferences are involved, we can further construct a set of indices by implementing regression and cosine distance. These indices plays the part of bricks in building a regression-based argumentation framework. In this part we first introduce the regression index ($\mathcal{RI}$) which represents the relation between the item in question and the overall situation of the data set. We then introduce the similarity index($\mathcal{SI}$) which tells us how similar two arguments are. In the argumentation framework to be defined, $\mathcal{RI}$ will be used as the base score of the arguments, and $\mathcal{SI}$ will be used as weights on the binary relations.

Definition 3.4 For a data set $\mathcal{D} = (d_0, d_1, ..., d_n)$, and a set of preferences $\mathcal{P} = \{p_1, p_2, ..., p_m\}$, we filter $\mathcal{D}$ using $\mathcal{P}$ to get a subset of $\mathcal{D}$, denoted as $\mathcal{D}[\mathcal{P}] = (d_{\mathcal{P}_0}, d_{\mathcal{P}_1}, \ldots, d_{\mathcal{P}_n})$. We do regression (linear, polynomial, stepwise, etc.) using the main column d_0 as an independent variable and $d_{\mathcal{P}_0}, d_{\mathcal{P}_1}, \ldots, d_{\mathcal{P}_n}$ as dependent variables, which gives to $\mathbf{Y} = f(\mathbf{X}) + \varepsilon$.
For the target item $\mathcal{I}$ with a dependent variable valued y_i and an error ε_i from the regression model, the *regression index* is $\mathcal{RI} = \frac{\varepsilon_i}{y_i}$.

The regression index shows how the actual value of dependent variable differs from its estimated value by regression. Here we use the ratio to present the difference in stead of immediately the error because it not only is more intuitive, but also normalizes the value and makes situations vary greatly in amount more comparable.

Then, we can define another index $\mathcal{SI}$ that describes the similarity between cases. In Section 2 we introduce the cosine distance S_{A-B} indicating the similarity between two agents' preferences. Based on the cosine similarity, we define an index that is more adaptable to argumentation frameworks.

Definition 3.5 The similarity index of two preference sets $\mathcal{P}_1, \mathcal{P}_2$ is $\mathcal{SI}(\mathcal{P}_1, \mathcal{P}_2) = \frac{S_{\mathcal{P}_1 - \mathcal{P}_2} - \xi}{1 - \xi}$, where $S_{\mathcal{P}_1 - \mathcal{P}_2}$ is the cosine distance between $\mathcal{P}_1, \mathcal{P}_2$ and ξ is a parameter that can be adjusted to fit into specific situations depending on the application.

We construct the index in this way to make sure that it is restricted to the range $(-\infty, 1]$, which facilitates a standard way of calculation. According to the above definition, $\mathcal{SI}$ can be either positive or negative depending on ξ's value. When $\mathcal{SI}$ is negative, we say that two cases on which arguments are based on are not similar and has no reference value. On the contrary, if $\mathcal{SI}$ is positive, then we say the two cases are similar enough, and one case should be taken into consideration when the decision concerning the other case is being made. But how similar is similar enough is dependent on t he context of application, so we make ξ a variable that is adjustable to various situations.

3.3 Weighted quantitative argumentation frameworks based on regression (W-QuAD)

Definition 3.6 A *weighted quantitative argumentation framework based on regression* is a 5-tuple $\mathcal{AF} = \langle \mathcal{A}, \mathcal{R}^+, \mathcal{R}^-, \mathcal{RI}, \mathcal{SI} \rangle$, where $\mathcal{A}$ is a set of data-preference-based arguments, $\mathcal{R}^+ \subseteq \mathcal{A} \times \mathcal{A}$ and $\mathcal{R}^- \subseteq \mathcal{A} \times \mathcal{A}$ are sets of binary relationships and $\mathcal{W}$ is a function from $\mathcal{R}^+ \cup \mathcal{R}^-$ to [0,1]. For $A_1 = \langle D_1, \mathcal{P}_1, \mathcal{T}_1 \rangle, A_2 = \langle D_2, \mathcal{P}_2, \mathcal{T}_2 \rangle \in \mathcal{A}$:

- $(A_1, A_2) \in \mathcal{R}^+$, if and only if $\mathcal{SI} > 0$, A_1 is a positive evidence for A_2, and A_1 precedes A_2 in terms of time;
- and $(A_1, A_2) \in \mathcal{R}^-$, if and only if $\mathcal{SI} > 0$, A_1 is a negative evidence for A_2, and A_1 precedes A_2 in terms of time.

Example 3.7 Suppose a customer c_1 preparing to buy a house H_1 with a set of preferences $\mathcal{P}_1$, after applying regression to houses on the market at present (D_1), the model finds that the regression index for H_1 is $\mathcal{I}_1 = 0.03$. Historically, we can find 2 successful and 2 failed deals, which yields 4 different arguments $\mathcal{A}_2 = \langle D_2, \mathcal{P}_2, \mathcal{T}_2 \rangle, \mathcal{A}_3 = \langle D_3, \mathcal{P}_3, \mathcal{T}_3 \rangle, \mathcal{A}_4 = \langle D_4, \mathcal{P}_4, \mathcal{T}_4 \rangle$, and $\mathcal{A}_5 = \langle D_5, \mathcal{P}_5, \mathcal{T}_5 \rangle$. The $\mathcal{RI}$s for $\mathcal{A}_2, \mathcal{A}_3, \mathcal{A}_4, \mathcal{A}_5$ are respectively $-0.02, 0.01, -0.015$, and 0.03. Deals succeed in $\mathcal{A}_2, \mathcal{A}_3$, and fail in $\mathcal{A}_4, \mathcal{A}_5$. Moreover, we assume the cosine similarity between $\mathcal{P}_1$ and $\mathcal{P}_2, \mathcal{P}_3, \mathcal{P}_4, \mathcal{P}_5$ to be 0.1, 0.3, 0.5 and 0.7 respectively. These five arguments, then, form a 2-layer quantitative bipolar argumentation framework based on data sets as presented by the graph below, with single arrows representing attacks, and double arrows representing supports.

Based on the argumentation framework we have defined, we can then stipulate the rules for choosing the house that is the most worth recommending. We do this by giving a recommendation score$\mathcal{RS}$ for argument on the second layer of argumentation framework.

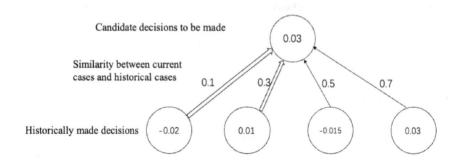

Fig. 2. 668-2

Definition 3.8 For a 2-layer quantitative bipolar argumentation framework based on data set, the recommendation score of an argument A_j on the second layer, and $A_1, A_2, ..., A_n$ arguments on the first layer, is $\mathcal{RS}(A_j) = -w_0\mathcal{RI}_j + \frac{1}{n}\sum_{i=1}^{n}\delta_{ij}\mathcal{SI}_{ij}\mathcal{RI}_i$, where w_0 is a parameter denoting the extent to which the current database is more important a reference than history records depending on the application.

To increase the probability of successful recommendation, the recommendation agent should recommend the instance with the highest score to the customer.

Example 3.9 Following last example with 4 arguments A_2, A_3, A_4, and A_5 on the history layer and 1 argument A_1 on the current layer, suppose $w_0 = 1$ in the case. Then, the recommendation score of argument A_1 gives to $\mathcal{RS}(A_1) = -0.03 + \frac{1}{4} \times [0.1 \times (-0.02) + 0.3 \times 0.01 - 0.5 \times (-0.015) - 0.7 \times 0.03] = 0.033125$. In the same way, if there are some other arguments on the current layer, we can repeat the process and calculate the recommendation score of them all. And by comparing these different scores, we can decide on which house to recommend to the house buyer. If there is more than one candidate for the decision (as shown by the figure above), we can repeat the process and calculate a recommendation score for every candidate.

4   Comparison with the Literature

Before our work on weighted argumentation framework, we notice that there are already some efforts to bridge the gap between human reasoning and recorded data in the existing literature. For instance, case-based reasoning [13,22], as a pronounced method of using old experiences to understand and solve new problems, combined with the ASPIC+ framework [16,9,23] well aligns the process of human reasoning based on precedents, especially in the legal field. Another pioneering work is matrix abduction developed by Gabbay et al. [14,5], which uses concepts of distances to derive topological knowledge graphs from numerical matrices. Lately, in computer science, argumentation has been

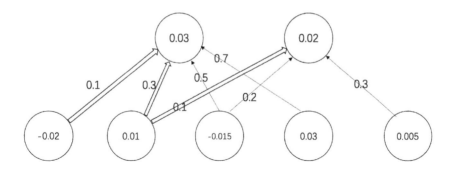

Fig. 3. 668-3

implemented to help provide explanations for interactive recommendation systems [12,17], specifying not only what items are recommended, but also why they are recommended. The above mentioned systems are different in character influence by the application areas they come and support. Our system comes from business area of buying and selling valuable items with buyer's preferences. The model is computed from objective data.

Our work takes a step further from the existing work trying to combine human reasoning with existing data. Compared with argumentative case-based reasoning and non-monotonic reasoning, it has a stronger ability to deal with numerical rather than quantitative data. It also relies less on the relative strengths of attributes or evidence than case-based reasoning does. In another light, our model can be considered as a development over the method of matrix abduction for it is more powerful and computationally simpler than previous distance-based methods when dealing with large data sets. Lastly, compared previous works trying to implement argumentation implemented in recommendation systems, it sheds new light for argumentation not only plays a part in providing explanations but also helps to make the recommendation more accurate.

Potential applications of our model are scenarios where the recommendation of items of the same kind is involved. The item can be some good on an online shopping platform, houses to be introduced to potential customers by the real estate agency, accommodation provided to travelers by the travel agency, and so on. This paper takes the house recommendation example as a typical case for illustration of the model.

5   Conclusion

In this paper we introduce a weighted quantitative argumentation framework based on regression, which is an extension of previous QuAD model.of Baroni et al [4]. The Baroni numerical values are essentially abstract (the strength of the argument is assigned through voting). Our model is based on real-life data in an actual application and shows how realistically the numerical values are calculated from the application and the strength of the attack and defense. For comparison, think of the theory of Generalised Coordinates in analytical mechanics as compared /applied to a real model like the motion of the planets in the solar system.

Our model implements the method of regression to assign base scores and method of cosine distance to assign weights to the attack or support relations between arguments. In practice, the model aligns a decision-making process where both real-time information and decisions made based on historical information are considered, and finds a way to make a decision taking account of both current and historical knowledge. We have seen a typical such application area in selling and buying houses.

However, there are some limitations of the model at the moment. First, the W-QuAD model is a two layer model and requires recalculation whenever a new argument is to be evaluated, which may add to the computational complexity. Second, to have the similarity index of the model and the generic score, it is not exactly clear how to get the parameter ξ and w_0, and how to decide whether the value of the parameter is optimal for the model.

There are many directions where discussion on this W-QuAD model can be improved. First, we may address the limitations of the model and find out ways to reduce computational complexity and find optimal parameters. Second, empirical studies based on the model may be designed to check how well it aligns with decision-making in practice and to what extent it contributes to an increase in more successful recommendations.This may require us to find a more testable example than a house purchase, for the data of house purchase is not very obtainable, and making a deal happen is too costly to be experimental. Instead of recommending houses, we may carry out experiments on recommending bubble teas to students to see how the model performs. For instance, we may make the price of bubble teas a dependent variable, and the tea, sugar, milk and other ingredients added to the tea independent variables. Such bubble tea behavior, then, can be tracked, and data can be collected to test the model. Moreover, as argumentation frameworks have a explanatory powers by nature, we can also further discuss how this model can be implemented not only in making a decision, but also in providing explanations.

References

[1] Amgoud, L., J. Ben-Naim, D. Doder and S. Vesic, *Acceptability semantics for weighted argumentation frameworks*, in: *Twenty-Sixth International Joint Conference on Artificial Intelligence*, 2017.

[2] Amgoud, L., C. Cayrol, M.-C. Lagasquie-Schiex and P. Livet, *On bipolarity in argumentation frameworks*, International Journal of Intelligent Systems **23** (2008), pp. 1062–1093.

[3] Baroni, P., D. Gabbay, M. Giacomin and L. Van der Torre, *Handbook of formal argumentation* (2018).

[4] Baroni, P., M. Romano, F. Toni, M. Aurisicchio and G. Bertanza, *Automatic evaluation of design alternatives with quantitative argumentation*, Argument & Computation **6**

(2015), pp. 24–49.

[5] Ben Adar Bessos, M. and D. M. Gabbay, *Topological aspects of matrix abduction 2*, in: *The Road to Universal Logic*, Springer, 2015 pp. 357–385.

[6] Cayrol, C. and M.-C. Lagasquie-Schiex, *On the acceptability of arguments in bipolar argumentation frameworks*, in: *European Conference on Symbolic and Quantitative Approaches to Reasoning and Uncertainty*, Springer, 2005, pp. 378–389.

[7] Coste-Marquis, S., S. Konieczny, P. Marquis and M. A. Ouali, *Selecting extensions in weighted argumentation frameworks.*, COMMA **12** (2012), pp. 342–349.

[8] Coste-Marquis, S., S. Konieczny, P. Marquis and M. A. Ouali, *Weighted attacks in argumentation frameworks*, in: *Thirteenth International Conference on the Principles of Knowledge Representation and Reasoning*, 2012.

[9] Cyras, K., K. Satoh and F. Toni, *Abstract argumentation for case-based reasoning*, in: *Fifteenth international conference on the principles of knowledge representation and reasoning*, 2016.

[10] Draper, N. R. and H. Smith, *Applied regression analysis* **326** (1998).

[11] Dung, P. M., *On the acceptability of arguments and its fundamental role in nonmonotonic reasoning, logic programming and n-person games*, Artificial intelligence **77** (1995), pp. 321–357.

[12] Ko, H., S. Lee, Y. Park and A. Choi, *A survey of recommendation systems: Recommendation models, techniques, and application fields*, Electronics **11** (2022), p. 141.

[13] Kolodner, J. L., *An introduction to case-based reasoning*, Artificial intelligence review **6** (1992), pp. 3–34.

[14] Laufer, A. and D. M. Gabbay, *Topological aspects of matrix abduction 1*, in: *The Road to Universal Logic*, Springer, 2015 pp. 339–355.

[15] Nouioua, F. and V. Risch, *Bipolar argumentation frameworks with specialized supports*, , **1**, IEEE, 2010, pp. 215–218.

[16] Prakken, H., A. Wyner, T. Bench-Capon and K. Atkinson, *A formalization of argumentation schemes for legal case-based reasoning in aspic+*, Journal of Logic and Computation **25** (2015), pp. 1141–1166.

[17] Rago, A., O. Cocarascu, C. Bechlivanidis, D. Lagnado and F. Toni, *Argumentative explanations for interactive recommendations*, Artificial Intelligence **296** (2021), p. 103506.

[18] Rago, A., F. Toni, M. Aurisicchio and P. Baroni, *Discontinuity-free decision support with quantitative argumentation debates*, in: *Fifteenth International Conference on the Principles of Knowledge Representation and Reasoning*, 2016.

[19] Rahutomo, F., T. Kitasuka and M. Aritsugi, *Semantic cosine similarity*, , **4**, 2012, p. 1.

[20] SIMARI, G. R., *Computation with varied-strength attacks in abstract argumentation frameworks*, Computational Models of Argument: Proceedings of COMMA 2010 **216** (2010), p. 207.

[21] Sykes, A. O., *An introduction to regression analysis* (1993).

[22] Watson, I. and F. Marir, *Case-based reasoning: A review*, The knowledge engineering review **9** (1994), pp. 327–354.

[23] Wyner, A. and T. Bench-Capon, *Argument schemes for legal case-based reasoning*, in: *JURIX*, Citeseer, 2007, pp. 139–149.

Strength and Accumulation of Evidence in Evidence-Based Argumentation Frameworks

Chen Chen, Beishui Liao

ZLAIRE, Zhejiang University, Hangzhou, China

Abstract

Evidence-based argumentation framework (EAF) is a special kind of bipolar argumentation framework in order to capture the notion of "evidential support". In an EAF, an argument cannot be accepted or be used to attack other arguments unless it is supported by evidence. However, different pieces of evidence may have different strengths, so arguments supported by different pieces of evidence may have different strengths. In this paper, we introduce a framework by extending an EAF with strength of evidence. Then, the strength of an argument is determined by the accumulation of the evidence supporting the argument. Moreover, the differences between this work and the study of argument accruals from the literature are discussed.

Keywords: strength of evidence, evidence based argumentation, accumulation.

1 Introduction

Formal argumentation has become a well-known paradigm for knowledge representation and reasoning with incomplete and inconsistent information [8]. Dung's abstract argumentation framework has greatly eased the modelling and study of argumentation. It consists of a collection of arguments interacting with each other through an attack relation, enabling to determine "acceptable" sets of arguments, called extensions. One important extension of Dung's argumentation frameworks is to allow positive interactions (usually expressed by a support relation) between arguments. There have been several different interpretations of support relation in the literature[15]. Among them, "evidential interpretation of support" deals with the relation between some evidence and a claim of an argument.

Evidence-based argumentation framework [16] is an extended abstract argumentation framework by adding evidential supports. It is intended to capture the notion of "support by evidence", meaning that an argument cannot be accepted unless it is supported by some evidence. In the framework, evidence is represented by a special type of arguments, called prima-facie arguments, and arguments can be accepted only if they are supported (directly or indirectly) by evidence.

However, in scientific and social practice, different kinds of evidence has different levels of strength. The evidence in medical diagnosis and treatment has several levels of strength[22]. Besides, Craig R. Fox studied how to assess strength of evidence from the perspective of cognitive psychology [9]. And, Berkman N. D. et al divided evidence in health care to several levels according to their strength[2]. It is obvious that arguments supported by strong evidence have higher strength than those supported by weaker evidence. This important notion has not been captured by the existing notion of evidence-based argumentation framework and leaves us some issues to study.

Level of evidence (LOE)	Description
Level I	Evidence from a systematic review or meta-analysis of all relevant RCTs (randomized controlled trial) or evidence-based clinical practice guidelines based on systematic reviews of RCTs or three or more RCTs of good quality that have similar results.
Level II	Evidence obtained from at least one well-designed RCT (e.g. large multi-site RCT).
Level III	Evidence obtained from well-designed controlled trials without randomization (i.e. quasi-experimental).
Level IV	Evidence from well-designed case-control or cohort studies.
Level V	Evidence from systematic reviews of descriptive and qualitative studies (meta-synthesis).
Level VI	Evidence from a single descriptive or qualitative study.
Level VII	Evidence from the opinion of authorities and/or reports of expert committees.

Fig. 1. This table from [1] illustrates different levels of evidence in the practice of nursing care according to their strength. Levels of evidence (sometimes called hierarchy of evidence) are assigned to studies based on the methodological quality of their design, validity, and applicability to patient care. These decisions gives the "grade (or strength) of recommendation".

The issue about how to determine strength of evidence or how to divide levels of evidence is not the main issue of this paper. What we want to do is actually to treat this phenomenon in computational argumentation. Based on the need of scientific practice, the research questions of this paper are:

(i) How to capture the notion of evidence strength?

(ii) How to model accumulation of evidence based on EAF?

This paper is organized as follows. Section 2 introduces and analyses evidence based argumentation. Section 3 models strength and accumulation of evidence in the new framework, namely evidence accumulation argumentation framework (ECAF). Several preliminary properties of ECAF will be given. Section 4 gives the conclusions of this paper and discusses the relation of ECAF and other formalisms in the literature.

2 Evidence based argumentation

Evidence-based argumentation is intended to capture the notion of evidential support: First, only supported arguments can be used to attack other arguments, while unsupported arguments will not be activated; Second, an argument cannot be accepted unless it is supported by some evidence. The initial version of evidence-based argumentation framework proposed by Oren and Norman [16] uses set attack and set support, which permit a set of arguments to attack/support one argument. Cayrol et al [4] proposed a simplified version that restricts the presentation of evidential support to the case where attacks and supports are carried out by single arguments. In this paper, for simplicity, we adopt the latter version.

Definition 2.1 [EAF] An evidence-based argumentation framework(EAF) is a tuple (A, E, R_{att}, R_{sup}), where A is a finite set of argument, $\emptyset \subset E \subset A$ is a set of prima-facie arguments representing evidence, $R_{att} \subseteq A \times (A \backslash E)$ is an attack relation, and $R_{sup} \subseteq A \times (A \backslash E)$ is a support relation such that $\nexists a, b \in A$: $(a, b) \in R_{att}$ and $(a, b) \in R_{sup}$.

Then, an evidential support (or e-support for short) can be defined as a particular case of the notion of (direct or indirect) support. Note that for simplicity, definitions in the rest of this section are all given in an EAF.

Definition 2.2 [e-Support] Given an EAF (A, E, R_{att}, R_{sup}), let $a \in A$, $S \subseteq A$.

- a is e-supported iff either $a \in E$ or there exists $b \in A$ such that b is e-supported and $(b, a) \in R_{sup}$.
- a is e-supported by S iff either $a \in E$ or there is an elementary sequence $b_1 R_{sup} \ldots R_{sup} b_n R_{sup} a$ such that $\{b_1 \ldots b_n\} \subseteq S$ and $b_1 \in E$.
- S is self-supporting iff S e-supports each of its elements.

Example 2.3 Consider $EAF = (A, E, R_{att}, R_{sup})$ where:

- $A = \{e_1, e_2, e_3, a, b\}$;
- $E = \{e_1, e_2, e_3\}$
- $att = \{(a, b), (b, a)\}$
- $sup = \{(e_1, a), (e_2, a), (e_3, b)\}$

In this framework, $\{e_1, a\}$ is a self-supporting set.

Only e-supported arguments are able to be used to make a direct attack on other arguments. This notion is formalized by e-supported attack.

Definition 2.4 [e-Supported attack] A set S is an e-supported attack on an argument a iff $\exists b \in S$, such that $(b, a) \in R_{att}$ and b is e-supported by S. A set

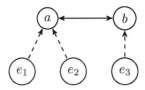

Fig. 2. Solid arrows denote attacks and dashed arrows denote supports

S is a minimal e-supported attack on an argument a iff S is an e-supported attack on a and $\nexists S' \subset S$ such that S' is an e-supported attack on a.

As a result of the notion "only e-supported arguments may be used to make a direct attack on other arguments", if an argument a is attacked by b, which is e-supported, a can be reinstated either by a direct attack on b or by an attack on c such that without c, b would be no longer e-supported. In order to implement this idea, notions of e-Acceptability and e-Admissibility are introduced as follows:

Definition 2.5 [e-Acceptability] Given an EAF (A, E, R_{att}, R_{sup}), let $a \in A$, $S \subseteq A$. We say that a is e-acceptable wrt S iff:

- For each minimal e-supported attack X on a, there exist $b \in S$ and $x \in X$ such that $b R_{att} x$ and

- b is e-supported by S.

Definition 2.6 [(e-Admissibility] Given an EAF (A, E, R_{att}, R_{sup}), let $S \subseteq A$. We say that S is e-admissible iff:

- Each element of S is e-acceptable wrt S, and

- there are no arguments $a, b \in S$, such that $a R_{att} b$.

Example 2.7 [ct'd example 2.3] $\{e_3, b\}$ is a minimal e-supported attack on a. a is acceptable with $\{e_1, e_2, a\}$. $\{e_1, e_2, a\}$ is admissible.

In an EAF, what matters to an argument is whether there exists evidence to e-support the argument. But, strength of evidence has no effect on the argument at all. This doesn't quite match our intuition about evidence. From a dynamic perspective, an argument becomes stronger if one finds more evidence to support it, and an argument becomes weaker if one finds some problems with some pieces of evidence supporting it (then some pieces of evidence will be removed from the framework).

3   Formalism

This section extends evidence-based argumentation with strength and accumulation of evidence.

Definition 3.1 [Evidence accumulation argumentation framework] An evidence accumulation argumentation framework (ECAF) is a 4-tuple $(A, E, R_{att}, R_{sup}, \preceq)$ where: A is a finite set of arguments; $E \subset A$ is a set of prima-facie arguments representing evidence; $R_{att} \subseteq (A \backslash E) \times (A \backslash E)$ is a symmetric relation representing attack; $R_{sup} \subseteq A \times (A \backslash E)$ represents direct support relation such that $\nexists a, b \in A$, $(a, b) \in R_{att}$ and $(a, b) \in R_{sup}$; $\preceq$ is a reflexive and transitive relation on 2^E such that $\forall E' \subseteq E, \{\} \preceq E'$. $\preceq$ is used to represent the preference relation over evidence. [1]

There are two points worth noting in an ECAF. First, attack relation is symmetric, because in this paper, for simplicity, we only consider rebutting relation between arguments, and in this definition the strength of individual arguments has not yet been taking into account. In [3], including undercutting relation in an EAF has been studied. To add undercutting relation into an ECAF can be done in the same way. We leave this to our future work. Second, preference relation is defined between sets of evidence rather than individual evidence. Based on attack relation and preference relation, defeat relation will be generated later in Definition 3.8.

Example 3.2 Consider an ECAF $\mathcal{F}_1 = (A, E, att, sup, \preceq)$ where:

- $A = \{e_1, e_2, e_3, e_4, a, b, c, d, f\}$;
- $E = \{e_1, e_2, e_3, e_4\}$
- $att = \{(a, b), (b, a), (d, f), (f, d)\}$
- $sup = \{(e_1, a), (e_2, b), (e_3, c), (e_4, f), (b, d), (c, d)\}$
- $\{e_1\} \preceq \{e_2\}$, $\{e_2\} \preceq \{e_1\}$, $\{e_2\} \preceq \{e_4\}$, $\{e_3\} \preceq \{e_4\}$, $\{e_4\} \preceq \{e_2, e_3\}$ and $\forall E'$ such that $\{\} \subset E' \subseteq E, \{\} \prec E'$.

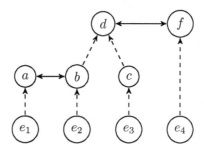

Fig. 3. Solid arrows denote attacks and dashed arrows denote supports

In this paper, we introduce the following two types of preference relation.

Definition 3.3 In an ECAF, the preference relation $\preceq$ is

- **increasing** iff for any $E_1, E_2, E_3 \subseteq E$, if $E_1 \preceq E_2$ then $E_1 \preceq E_2 \cup E_3$;
- **flat** iff for any non-empty sets $E_1, E_2 \subseteq E$, $E_1 \preceq E_2$ and $E_2 \preceq E_1$.

An increasing preference relation means that adding new evidence to a set either enhances or maintains, but cannot weaken, its strength. And a flat preference relation means that every set of evidence has the same preference.

---

[1] $E_1 \prec E_2$ iff $E_1 \preceq E_2$ and $E_2 \npreceq E_1$

Given an ECAF, we use labelling to represent the acceptability status of arguments, and evidence base to represent the strength of an argument determined by some evidence that successfully supports the argument.

Definition 3.4 [Labelling] Given an ECAF $\mathcal{F} = (A, E, R_{att}, R_{sup}, \preceq)$, a labelling L of $\mathcal{F}$ is any pair of non-overlapping subsets $(in(L), out(L))$ of A. The set of all labellings of $\mathcal{F}$ is denoted $\mathcal{L}(\mathcal{F})$.

A labelling L divides arguments into three parts: to be accepted $(in(L))$, to be rejected $(out(L))$ and undecided (not in $in(L)$ or $out(L)$). Evidence arguments are all labelled in because evidence is considered deadly right and must be accepted unconditionally. To illustrate this definition in Example 3.2, $(\{e_1, e_2, e_3, e_4, a, c, d\}, \{b, f\})$ is a labelling of $\mathcal{F}_1$.

In our approach, arguments' strength is determined by the evidence used successfully to support it. The evidence base of an argument a is a set of evidence used to support a. So, evidence base is defined on the basis of a given labelling. This method is called Recursive labelling [19]. If an argument is labelled out, then this argument cannot be used to support anything. In other words, it cannot appear in any argument's evidence base.

Definition 3.5 [Evidence base] Given an ECAF $\mathcal{F} = (A, E, R_{att}, R_{sup}, \preceq)$ and a labelling L of A, a set $E' \subseteq E$ is an evidence base of an argument $a \in A$, denoted $base(a)$, iff it satisfies both of the following conditions:

(i) for any $e \in E$, if $e \in base(a)$ then there is a sequence $eR_{sup}a_1R_{sup}\ldots R_{sup}a_nR_{sup}a$ such that $a_1, \ldots, a_n$ are not labelled out;

(ii) for any $e \in E$, if there is a sequence $eR_{sup}a_1R_{sup}\ldots R_{sup}a_nR_{sup}a$ such that $a_1, \ldots, a_n$ are labelled in, then $e \in base(a)$.

In Definition 3.5, the first condition states the necessary condition for a piece of evidence to be in the evidence base of an argument: if evidence e is in $base(a)$, then e is in a set of arguments that are not labelled out to support a. Condition 2 states the sufficient condition for a piece of evidence to be in an accrual: if evidence e is in a set of arguments all labelled in to support an argument a, then e must be in the accruals of a.

We use $EB(\mathcal{F}, L) = \{base(a) \mid a \in A\}$ to denote the set of evidence bases of $\mathcal{F}$ in terms of L.

Example 3.6 (ct'd Example 3.2)

- given a labelling $(\{e_1, e_2, e_3, e_4, b\}, \{a\})$, then argument d has two evidence bases: $\{e_2, e_3\}$ and $\{e_2\}$. We can see that there is a sequence $e_2R_{sup}bR_{sup}d$ such that e_2 and b are labelled in, so e_2 is in every evidence bases of d. Also, e_3 can be in the evidence base of d because there is a sequence $e_3R_{sup}cR_{sup}d$ such that c is not labelled out.

- given a labelling $(\{e_1, e_2, e_3, e_4, a\}, \{b, c\})$, then argument d does not have any evidence base except $\{\}$ because every sequence supporting d has at least one piece labelled out.

Lemma 3.7 *Let L be a labelling of an ECAF $(A, E, R_{att}, R_{sup}, \preceq)$. Any argument $a \in A$ has at least one evidence base which can be an empty set.*

Proof. Let $S = \{e \in E \mid$ there is a sequence $eR_{sup}a_1R_{sup} \ldots R_{sup}a_nR_{sup}a$ such that $a_1, \ldots, a_n$ are not labelled *out*$\}$ and $S' = \{e \in E \mid$there is a sequence $eR_{sup}a_1R_{sup} \ldots R_{sup}a_nR_{sup}a$ such that $a_1, \ldots, a_n$ are labelled *in*$\}$. Then, for all $S'' \in 2^S$, according to Definition 3.5, $S' \cup S''$ is an evidence base of a. Besides, if $S = S' = \{\}$, then there is only one $base(a)$, that is $\{\}$. As a result, a has at least one evidence base. $\qquad\Box$

Evidence base illustrates the strength of arguments. As a result, we may compare two conflicting arguments through their evidence bases. If arguments a and b conflict with each other, then a defeats b if one of a's evidence bases is not weaker than one of b's evidence bases.

Definition 3.8 [Defeat] Given an ECAF $\mathcal{F} = (A, E, R_{att}, R_{sup}, \preceq)$, a labelling $L = (in(L), out(L))$ of $\mathcal{F}$, and the set of evidence base $EB(\mathcal{F}, L)$. Argument $a \in A$ **defeats** argument $b \in A$ iff:

(i) $(a, b) \in R_{att}$, and

(ii) for some $base(a), base(b) \in EB(\mathcal{F}, L)$, it holds that $base(a) \not\preceq base(b)$.

Example 3.9 (ct'd Example 3.6) Given a labelling $(\{e_1, e_2, e_3, e_4\}, \{\})$ of $\mathcal{F}_1$, a has only one evidence base: $\{e_1\}$, and b also has only one evidence base: $\{e_2\}$. Because $\{e_1\} \preceq \{e_2\}$ and $\{e_2\} \preceq \{e_1\}$, a and b defeat each other. Given a labelling $(\{e_1, e_2, e_3, e_4, c\}, \{\})$, d has two evidence bases: $\{e_2, e_3\}$ and $\{e_3\}$, f has one evidence base: $\{e_4\}$. Because $\{e_3\} \preceq \{e_4\}$ and $\{e_4\} \preceq \{e_2, e_3\}$, d and f defeat each other.

Next, we introduce the notion of complete labelling in ECAF to define argument evaluation recursively.

Definition 3.10 [Complete labelling] Let $\mathcal{F} = (A, E, R_{att}, R_{sup}, \preceq)$ be an ECAF. The characteristic function of $\mathcal{F}$ is a total function $F : \mathcal{L}(\mathcal{F}) \to \mathcal{L}(\mathcal{F})$. For all $L \in \mathcal{L}(\mathcal{F})$, for all $a \in A$, the following conditions are satisfied:

(i) $a \in in(F(L))$ iff:
   - $a \in E$ or there is a sequence $eR_{sup}a_1R_{sup} \ldots R_{sup}a_nR_{sup}a$ such that $e \in E$ and $a_1, \ldots, a_n$ are labelled $in(L)$; and
   - $\forall b$ defeats a, $b \in out(L)$; and

(ii) $a \in out(F(L))$ iff:
   - $a \notin E$ and there isn't a sequence $eR_{sup}a_1R_{sup} \ldots R_{sup}a_nR_{sup}a$ such that $e \in E$ and $a_1, \ldots, a_n$ are not labelled $out(L)$; or
   - $\exists b$ defeats a, $b \in in(L)$.

A **complete labelling** of $\mathcal{F}$ is any fixpoint of F.

Definition 3.11 [Grounded labelling] Let $\mathcal{F} = (A, E, R_{att}, R_{sup}, \preceq)$ be an ECAF. A complete labelling $L = (in(L), out(L))$ of $\mathcal{F}$ is a grounded labelling iff $in(L)$ is minimal (w.r.t set inclusion) among all complete labellings of $\mathcal{F}$.

Definition 3.12 [Preferred labelling] Let $\mathcal{F} = (A, E, R_{att}, R_{sup}, \preceq)$ be an ECAF. A complete labelling $L = (in(L), out(L))$ of $\mathcal{F}$ is a preferred labelling iff $in(L)$ is maximal (w.r.t set inclusion) among all complete labellings of $\mathcal{F}$.

Definition 3.13 [Stable labelling] Let $\mathcal{F} = (A, E, R_{att}, R_{sup}, \preceq)$ be an ECAF. A complete labelling $L = (in(L), out(L))$ of $\mathcal{F}$ is a stable labelling iff $in(L) \cup out(L) = A$.

Example 3.14 (ct'd Example 3.2) $\mathcal{F}_1$ has five complete labellings:

- $L_1 = (\{e_1, e_2, e_3, e_4, c\}, \{\})$;
- $L_2 = (\{e_1, e_2, e_3, e_4, c, d\}, \{f\})$;
- $L_3 = (\{e_1, e_2, e_3, e_4, c, f\}, \{d\})$;
- $L_4 = (\{e_1, e_2, e_3, e_4, c, a, f\}, \{b, d\})$;
- $L_5 = (\{e_1, e_2, e_3, e_4, c, b, d\}, \{a, f\})$.

Among these complete labellings, L_1 is a grounded labelling, L_4 and L_5 are preferred labellings and stable labellings.

By definition, all preferred, grounded and stable labellings are complete labellings.

Finally, for $\sigma \in \{\text{complete, preferred, grounded, stable}\}$, an argument is sceptically or credulously justified if it is labelled *in* by all, respectively at least one, σ labelling.

Next, several properties of ECAF are given as follows.

Proposition 3.15 *For $\sigma \in \{complete, preferred, grounded, stable\}$, $\forall e \in E$, e is sceptically justified.*

Proof. Let $e \in E$ be a piece of evidence. For any complete labelling L, $L = F(L)$. According to Definition 3.10, $e \in in(F(L))$ because $e \in E$. Then $e \in in(L)$. As a result, e is labelled *in* by all complete labellings. Because all preferred, grounded and stable labellings are also complete labellings, e is labelled *in* by all preferred, grounded and stable labellings. So for all $\sigma \in \{\text{complete, preferred, grounded, stable}\}$, $\forall e \in E$, e is sceptically justified. $\square$

Proposition 3.16 *Let $\mathcal{F} = (A, E, R_{att}, R_{sup}, \preceq)$ be an ECAF. For all $\sigma \in \{complete, preferred, grounded, stable\}$, $\forall a \in A$, if for all $b \in A$ such that $bR_{sup}a$, b is not credulously justified, then a is not credulously justified.*

Proof. Assume that $a \in A$ is credulously justified, and for all $b \in A$ such that $bR_{sup}a$, b is not credulously justified. For $\sigma \in \{\text{complete, preferred, grounded, stable}\}$, because a is credulously justified, there exists a σ labelling L such that $a \in in(L)$. Because for all b such that $bR_{sup}a$, b is not credulously justified, $b \notin in(L)$. As a result, there does not exist a sequence $eR_{sup}a_1R_{sup}\ldots R_{sup}a_nR_{sup}a$ such that $e \in E$ and $a_1, \ldots, a_n \in in(L)$. According to Definition 3.10, $a \notin in(F(L))$. In other words, L is not a fixpoint of F, so L is not a complete labelling. Because a preferred, grounded and stable labelling is a complete labelling, L is not a σ labelling. This contradicts the assumption. So, a is not credulously justified. $\square$

Proposition 3.16 says that if an argument has no supporter to be credulously justified, the argument itself will also not be credulously justified.

There are still some other important properties of ECAF, especially about dynamics. For example if $\preceq$ is increasing, adding an argument a to support an argument b into the framework will at least not weaken b. And reversely, if $\preceq$ is decreasing, adding an argument a to support an argument b into the framework will at least not strengthen b. Due to the limitation of the paper, these properties will be presented formally in our future work.

4   Conclusion and discussion

This paper extends evidence-based argumentation framework with strength and accumulation of evidence. The motivation is clear: evidence in practice differs in strength, and evidence may accumulate to support an argument. The core concept in this paper is evidence base. For a single argument, its evidence bases are influenced by the whole labelling of the framework. The defeat relation and argument evaluation also rely on evidence bases of arguments. Next, we compare ECAF with other notions in the literature.

In computational argumentation, accrual proposed by Pollock[17] means several arguments which are on their own defeated but together remain undefeated [21]. Prakken[18] set three principles for any formalisms modelling argument accruals to follow: First, an accrual is sometimes weaker than its accruing elements. Second, an accrual makes its elements inapplicable. Third, flawed arguments should not accrue. Accrual is modelled in ASPIC$^+$[19], DeLP[13,10,14] and strength-based abstract argumentation[20]. The main differences between ECAF and accrual are: First, ECAF models strength and accumulation of evidence, and accrual acts directly on arguments. Second, they are on different levels of argumentation, namely structured level and abstract level. Specially, the work to model accrual in abstract argumentation[20] differs from ECAF in terms of framework and semantics very much.

This paper presents a preliminary work on strength and accumulation of evidence in argumentation frameworks. Future work includes: First, the semantics of an ECAF in this paper is complicated, we want to introduce the incremental computation[11] method to ECAF. It's not difficult to see that arguments in an ECAF have clear levels. To illustrate this in Example 3.2, before dealing with the conflict between d and f, the conflict between a and b should be settled first. If a defeats b but not vice versa, then b will be "out" and e_2 won't be in d's evidence base. Then, we could deal with d and f accordingly, namely d is defeated by f. Second, we are going to model strength and accumulation of evidence in recursive argumentation frameworks [5], which allow relations (support and attack) to be attacked. As a result, something similar to "undercut" in structured argumentation frameworks are introduced into our new framework. The last is to study the aggregation [6], dynamics [12] and control [7] of ECAF.

5 Acknowledgement

We would like to thank three anonymous reviewers for their helpful comments. Besides, this work has received funding from the Natural Science Foundation of Zhejiang Province under Grant Number LY20F030014 and the Key Program of the National Social Science Foundation of China, No. 20&ZD047.

References

[1] Ackley, B., B. Swan, G. Ladwig and S. Tucker, *Evidence-based nursing care guidelines: Medical-surgical interventions; mosby elsevier: St,* Louis, MI, USA (2008), p. 7.

[2] Berkman, N. D., K. N. Lohr, M. Ansari, M. McDonagh, E. Balk, E. Whitlock, J. Reston, E. Bass, M. Butler, G. Gartlehner et al., *Grading the strength of a body of evidence when assessing health care interventions for the effective health care program of the agency for healthcare research and quality: an update* (2014).

[3] Cayrol, C., J. Fandinno, L. Fariñas del Cerro and M.-C. Lagasquie-Schiex, *Argumentation frameworks with recursive attacks and evidence-based supports,* in: *International Symposium on Foundations of Information and Knowledge Systems,* Springer, 2018, pp. 150–169.

[4] Cayrol, C. and M.-C. Lagasquie-Schiex, *Bipolarity in argumentation graphs: Towards a better understanding,* International Journal of Approximate Reasoning **54** (2013), pp. 876–899.

[5] Cohen, A., S. Gottifredi, A. J. García and G. R. Simari, *An approach to abstract argumentation with recursive attack and support,* Journal of Applied Logic **13** (2015), pp. 509–533.

[6] Delobelle, J., S. Konieczny and S. Vesic, *On the aggregation of argumentation frameworks,* in: *Twenty-Fourth International Joint Conference on Artificial Intelligence,* 2015.

[7] Dimopoulos, Y., J.-G. Mailly and P. Moraitis, *Control argumentation frameworks,* , **32**, 2018.

[8] Dung, P. M., *On the acceptability of arguments and its fundamental role in nonmonotonic reasoning, logic programming and n-person games,* Artificial intelligence **77** (1995), pp. 321–357.

[9] Fox, C. R., *Strength of evidence, judged probability, and choice under uncertainty,* Cognitive Psychology **38** (1999), pp. 167–189.

[10] Gómez Lucero, M. J., C. I. Chesnevar and G. R. Simari, *Modelling argument accrual in possibilistic defeasible logic programming,* in: *European Conference on Symbolic and Quantitative Approaches to Reasoning and Uncertainty,* Springer, 2009, pp. 131–143.

[11] Liao, B., *Toward incremental computation of argumentation semantics: A decomposition-based approach,* Annals of Mathematics and Artificial Intelligence **67** (2013), pp. 319–358.

[12] Liao, B., L. Jin and R. C. Koons, *Dynamics of argumentation systems: A division-based method,* Artificial Intelligence **175** (2011), pp. 1790–1814.

[13] Lucero, M. J. G., C. I. Chesñevar and G. R. Simari, *On the accrual of arguments in defeasible logic programming,* in: *Twenty-First International Joint Conference on Artificial Intelligence,* 2009.

[14] Lucero, M. J. G., C. I. Chesñevar and G. R. Simari, *Modelling argument accrual with possibilistic uncertainty in a logic programming setting,* Information Sciences **228** (2013), pp. 1–25.

[15] Nouioua, F. and V. Risch, *Bipolar argumentation frameworks with specialized supports,* , **1**, IEEE, 2010, pp. 215–218.

[16] Oren, N. and T. Norman, *Semantics for evidence-based argumentation,* in: *Proceedings of the 2008 Computational Models of Argument* (2008), pp. 276–284.

[17] Pollock, J. L., *Self-defeating arguments,* Minds and Machines **1** (1991), pp. 367–392.

[18] Prakken, H., *A study of accrual of arguments, with applications to evidential reasoning*, in: *Proceedings of the Tenth International Conference on Artificial Intelligence and Law*, 2005, pp. 85–94.

[19] Prakken, H., *Modelling accrual of arguments in aspic+*, in: *Proceedings of the seventeenth international conference on artificial intelligence and law*, 2019, pp. 103–112.

[20] Rossit, J., J.-G. Mailly, Y. Dimopoulos and P. Moraitis, *United we stand: Accruals in strength-based argumentation*, Argument & Computation **12** (2021), pp. 87–113.

[21] Verheij, B., *Accrual of arguments in defeasible argumentation*, in: *Proceedings of the Second Dutch/German Workshop on Nonmonotonic Reasoning*, 1995, p. 217–224.

[22] Wright, J. G., M. F. Swiontkowski and J. D. Heckman, *Introducing levels of evidence to the journal* (2003).

Higher-order Logic as a Lingua Franca for Logico-Pluralist Argumentation

David Fuenmayor [1]

University of Luxembourg & University of Bamberg & Freie Universität Berlin

Christoph Benzmüller

University of Bamberg & Freie Universität Berlin

Abstract

Thanks to its expressivity, higher-order logic can adopt the status of a uniform *lingua franca* allowing the logico-pluralist formalization of arguments (i.e. their deep logical structure) and their dialectical interactions (attack and support relations). A novel contribution of this work concerns the language-theoretical characterization of the technique of *shallow semantical embeddings* of non-classical logics in higher-order logic (as a universal meta-logic), which constitute a pillar stone of the LogiKEy knowledge engineering framework and methodology. This novel perspective enables more concise and more elegant characterizations of semantical embeddings of logics and logic combinations, which is demonstrated with several examples.

Keywords: knowledge representation, argumentation, logical pluralism, higher-order logic, shallow embedding.

1 Introduction

The need for combining heterogeneous, expressive logical formalisms for the analysis of argumentative discourse is manifest in view of the richness of natural language phenomena. In our view, the problem is less the lack of logical systems to represent those diverse perspectives, but rather the issue of bringing them coherently under the same roof. In other words, what is actually lacking is a *lingua franca* by means of which we can (i) flexibly combine logics, as required, e.g., for the formalization of non-trivial normative arguments, and (ii) enable the articulation of inter-logical dialectical relations: *how can arguments formalized using different logics actually attack or support each other?*

The proposed solution relies on the adoption of classical higher-order logic *as a metalanguage* into which the logical connectives of (a combination of) object logics can be 'translated' or 'embedded'. This approach, termed *shallow*

---

[1] The author acknowledges support by the Luxembourg National Research Fund (FNR), project AuReLeE (Automated Reasoning with Legal Entities) [Grant: C20/IS/14616644].

semantical embeddings (SSE) [2,7], has quite interesting practical applications, as it fosters the reuse of existing reasoning infrastructure for first- and higher-order logic for seamlessly combining and reasoning with different quantified classical and non-classical logics—including modal, deontic, and paraconsistent logics as illustrated below—many of which are well suited for normative reasoning applications. The SSE technique has thus become the pillar stone of the LogiKEy [6] framework and methodology for designing normative theories in ethical and legal reasoning, as it supports a *logico-pluralistic* approach towards the formalization of arguments, indeed blurring the line between logical and extralogical (resp. syncategorematic and categorematic) expressions.

An illustrative situation is depicted in Fig. 1, where two arguments, formalized in, say, logics $\mathbf{L}_1$ and $\mathbf{L}_2$, jointly attack a third argument, formalized in logic $\mathbf{L}_3$. This attack can itself be modeled as an argument encoded in the logic combination $\mathbf{L}_1 \oplus \mathbf{L}_2 \oplus \mathbf{L}_3$. Notice that, in non-trivial cases, there is a need for additional, tacit premises (P_T in Fig. 1), which can have a different nature. They can be definitions for the connectives of the object logic (cf. §3). Some may be part of underlying (meta-)logical theories, and thus correspond to axioms (such as modal

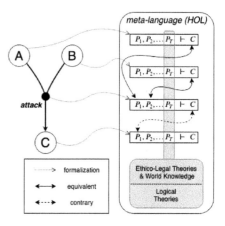

Fig. 1: A joint undermining attack.

K, D, 4, etc.), or their corresponding semantical constraints (cf. modal *correspondence theory*), while others may correspond to formalized principles from, e.g., domain theories or world knowledge (cf. [6, §7.2]). They may also correspond to contextual, 'implicit' assumptions specific to the current debate.

We introduce a conceptual framework in §2-§3 allowing us to better articulate theoretically our notion of SSE; we draw upon these notions, in §4, to propose a logico-pluralist approach towards encoding structured arguments in higher-order logic. We conclude in §5 and discuss further work and prospects.

2   Signatures and Languages

It is customary to define propositional languages over a given set of propositional symbols (sometimes called a 'signature'), while the logical connectives are introduced by the language-generating mechanism or grammar. As an illustration, a typical textbook approach for defining a modal language starts by introducing a 'signature' $\mathcal{P} = \{p^n\}_{0 \leq n < m}$ consisting of m propositional atoms. Subsequently, the modal language becomes defined inductively by a grammar such as the following, where p ranges over elements of $\mathcal{P}$:

$$\varphi := p \mid \bot \mid \neg\varphi \mid \varphi_1 \vee \varphi_2 \mid \Box\varphi.$$

By contrast, presenting a logico-pluralistic approach compels us to do things slightly differently. Our main tactic in this section consists in shifting logical connectives from the grammar into the signature of a language, which is a principle particularly well known in the literature on higher-order logics. This move facilitates definitions and assessments at a higher level of abstraction.

Before getting started some remarks are pertinent: The present section aims at building a conceptual framework and is thus rich in definitions. For each of them we have provided one or several examples regarding well-known modal-like systems, many of which have been previously encoded using the SSE approach (see e.g. the examples at `logikey.org`). It is important to note that SSEs of non-modal systems are also possible (e.g. [19]) though less studied. In this exposition we strive for a middle path between readability and rigor. For convenience, we may switch between prefix and infix notation for connectives, and we may omit parentheses when they can be easily inferred from the context.

2.1 Propositional Signatures

We start with discussing propositional languages since, in spite of their simplicity, they readily provide a suitable conceptual bridge towards the sort of functional higher-order languages we utilize in the SSE approach. We will gracefully skip first-order logic, since, for practical purposes, formulating first-order languages as fragments of an adequate higher-order language suffices.

Definition 2.1 [P-Signature] A propositional signature (abbrev. *P-signature*) is a tuple $\mathcal{S} = \langle \mathcal{C}, \mathcal{P}_0 \rangle$, where $\mathcal{C}$ is a non-empty, denumerable set of disjoint sets $\{\mathcal{C}_k\}_{k \in \mathbb{N}}$, and $\mathcal{P}_0$ is a possibly empty, denumerable set $\{p^n\}_{n \in \mathbb{N}}$. The elements of each $\mathcal{C}_k$ are symbols called *k-ary* connectives and are always given a fixed (intended) interpretation. The elements of $\mathcal{P}_0$ are called *propositional symbols* (or *parameters*) and their denotation varies in each interpretation.

$\mathcal{C}$ and $\mathcal{P}_0$ can be seen as *logical*, resp. *extralogical*, base expressions of a propositional language, and elements of $\mathcal{P}_0$ can be seen as having arity zero. In the sequel, to avoid cluttering in our notation, all sets $\mathcal{C}_k$ which are not explicitly mentioned are assumed to be empty. Union and intersection of signatures is defined component-wise, e.g., $\mathcal{S}^1 \cup \mathcal{S}^2 = \langle \{\mathcal{C}_k\}_{k \in \mathbb{N}}, \mathcal{P}_0 \rangle$, with $\mathcal{C}_k = \mathcal{C}_k^1 \cup \mathcal{C}_k^2$ and $\mathcal{P}_0 = \mathcal{P}_0^1 \cup \mathcal{P}_0^2$. Signatures can be minimal or non-minimal.

Example 2.2 [CPL] An example P-signature for classical propositional logic (CPL) with m propositional symbols is: $\mathcal{S}_{\mathrm{CPL}} = \langle \{\mathcal{C}_1, \mathcal{C}_2\}, \{p^n\}_{n < m} \rangle$, with $\mathcal{C}_1 = \{\neg\}$ and $\mathcal{C}_2 = \{\wedge\}$. Observe that $\mathcal{S}_{\mathrm{CPL}}$ is a minimal signature.

Example 2.3 [ML] An example P-signature for multi-modal propositional logic with denumerable propositional symbols is: $\mathcal{S}_{\mathrm{ML}} = \langle \{\mathcal{C}_1, \mathcal{C}_2\}, \{p^n\}_{n \in \mathbb{N}} \rangle$, with $\mathcal{C}_1 = \{\neg\} \cup \{\Box^n\}_{n \in \mathbb{N}}$ and $\mathcal{C}_2 = \{\wedge\}$.

2.2 Propositional Languages

In the present approach, languages are not simply sets of well-formed formulas. They must be generated inductively by a signature. In addition to the signature symbols, we assume a fixed, denumerable set $\mathcal{V}_0 = \{v^n\}_{n \in \mathbb{N}}$ of schema variables.

Definition 2.4 [P-Language] The propositional language (abbrv. *P-language*) $\mathcal{L}^P(\mathcal{S})$ over the P-signature $\mathcal{S} = \langle\{\mathcal{C}_k\}_{k\in\mathbb{N}}, \mathcal{P}_0\rangle$ is the smallest set such that:

(i) $v, p, c \in \mathcal{L}^P(\mathcal{S})$ for every $v \in \mathcal{V}_0$, $p \in \mathcal{P}_0$, and $c \in \mathcal{C}_0$;

(ii) $c(\varphi_1, \ldots, \varphi_k) \in \mathcal{L}^P(\mathcal{S})$, whenever $c \in \mathcal{C}_k$ ($k \geq 1$) and $\varphi_1, \ldots, \varphi_k \in \mathcal{L}^P(\mathcal{S})$.

Example 2.5 Each P-signature $\mathcal{S}$ presented in Ex. 2.2–2.3 induces a corresponding *P-language* $\mathcal{L}^P(\mathcal{S})$ in the manner exposed above.

Definition 2.6 [Language Fragment] Let $\mathcal{L}^1$ and $\mathcal{L}^2$ be two languages, i.e., there exist signatures $\mathcal{S}^1$ and $\mathcal{S}^2$ such that $\mathcal{L}^1 = \mathcal{L}^P(\mathcal{S}^1)$ and $\mathcal{L}^2 = \mathcal{L}^P(\mathcal{S}^2)$. We say that $\mathcal{L}^1$ is a *fragment* of $\mathcal{L}^2$, and write $\mathcal{L}^1 \leq \mathcal{L}^2$, iff $\mathcal{L}^1 \subseteq \mathcal{L}^2$. The above characterization is indeed applicable to any language induced by a signature.

Example 2.7 Language $\mathcal{L}^P(\mathcal{S}_{\text{CPL}})$ is a fragment of language $\mathcal{L}^P(\mathcal{S}_{\text{ML}})$.

It is worth noting that presentations of propositional languages often include so-called *derived connectives*, which are in fact abbreviations ('syntactic sugar') for sequences of connectives; e.g., in modal logics the operator $\Diamond$ often abbreviates $\neg\Box\neg$. Note, however, that $\neg\Box\neg$ is not a well-formed expression, and thus there is no proper way to characterize derived connectives using P-signatures and the language-generating grammar presented above. This contrasts with higher-order languages, introduced in Section 2.4, which are equipped with a suitable functional abstraction mechanism that can be used for this purpose.

2.3   Higher-order Signatures

We now introduce higher-order, functional signatures as a straightforward generalization of *P-signatures*.

Definition 2.8 [Functional Type] We inductively define the set τ of *functional types*, which play an analogous role to arities in P-signatures:

$$\iota_n \in \tau \quad \text{for every} \quad n \in \mathbb{N}; \qquad \alpha{\rightarrow}\beta \in \tau, \quad \text{whenever} \quad \alpha, \beta \in \tau.$$

We use the following aliases for commonly used (base) types: o for ι_0, w for ι_1, and e for ι_2. Note that $\rightarrow$ associates to the right, so that $\alpha{\rightarrow}\beta{\rightarrow}\gamma$ is shorthand for $\alpha{\rightarrow}(\beta{\rightarrow}\gamma)$. Moreover, $\alpha^n{\rightarrow}\beta$ is shorthand for $\alpha{\rightarrow}\alpha{\rightarrow}\cdots$ (n-times) $\cdots{\rightarrow}\beta$.

We do not introduce product types, since they can (and will) be emulated using functional types. For example, the product type $(\alpha \times \beta){\rightarrow}\eta$ corresponds to the functional type $\alpha{\rightarrow}(\beta{\rightarrow}\eta)$. [2]

Definition 2.9 [F-Signature] A functional signature (abbrv. *F-signature*) is a pair $\mathcal{S} = \langle\mathcal{C}, \mathcal{P}\rangle$, where $\mathcal{C}$ is a non-empty denumerable set of disjoint sets $\{\mathcal{C}_\alpha\}_{\alpha\in\tau}$, and where $\mathcal{P}$ is a (possibly empty) denumerable set of disjoint sets $\{\mathcal{P}_\alpha\}_{\alpha\in\tau}$. The elements of each $\mathcal{C}_\alpha$ are called *connectives* of type α and are

---

[2]   As an illustration, in a functional language, a binary operator such as $+ : \mathbb{N}\times\mathbb{N}{\rightarrow}\mathbb{N}$ acquires the type: $\mathbb{N}{\rightarrow}(\mathbb{N}{\rightarrow}\mathbb{N})$. Thus, an expression such as, e.g., "3 + 4" becomes formalized as $((+\ 3)\ 4)$ (infix notation can always be reintroduced as 'syntactic sugar' though). The notion underlying these phenomena is known as *Schönfinkelization* or *Currying* in the literature.

always given a fixed 'intended' interpretation. The elements of each $\mathcal{P}_\alpha$ are *functional symbols* (or *parameters*) of type α. Their interpretation is not fixed.

Note that *F-signatures* do not feature λ-expressions, which appear instead in the grammar (cf. Def. 2.16). Thus, by keeping the grammar fixed, differences in the defined languages can only be due to changes in the signature.

For the present purposes our exposition focuses on syntactic aspects only. As for semantics, we restrict ourselves to noting that for every type $\gamma \in \tau$ we assume a non-empty set $\mathcal{D}_\gamma$ as its semantic domain, and symbols of type $\alpha \to \beta$ are intended to denote functions from $\mathcal{D}_\alpha$ into $\mathcal{D}_\beta$ (i.e. $\lceil \varphi_{\alpha \to \beta} \rceil : \mathcal{D}_\alpha \to \mathcal{D}_\beta$).

Example 2.10 [CPL-F] An example *F-signature* for CPL with m propositional symbols is: $\mathcal{S}_{\text{CPL-F}} = \langle \{\mathcal{C}_{o \to o}, \mathcal{C}_{o \to o \to o}\}, \{\mathcal{P}_o\}\rangle$, with $\mathcal{C}_{o \to o} = \{\neg\}$, $\mathcal{C}_{o \to o \to o} = \{\wedge\}$ and $\mathcal{P}_o = \{p^n\}_{n < m}$. (Compare with the P-signature in Ex. 2.2.)

Note that type o is intended to represent truth-values, and types $o \to o$ and $o \to o \to o$ are intended to represent unary resp. binary logical connectives.

Example 2.11 [FOL] An example *F-signature* for first-order logic with equality, countably many function symbols, m individual 'constants', and n unary predicates is: $\mathcal{S}_{\text{FOL-F}} = \langle \{\mathcal{C}_{o \to o}, \mathcal{C}_{o \to o \to o}, \mathcal{C}_{e \to e}, \mathcal{C}_{e \to e \to o}, \mathcal{C}_{(e \to o) \to o}\}, \{\mathcal{P}_e, \mathcal{P}_{e \to o}\}\rangle$, with $\mathcal{C}_{o \to o} = \{\neg\}$, $\mathcal{C}_{o \to o \to o} = \{\wedge, \vee, \to\}$, $\mathcal{C}_{e \to e} = \{f^k\}_{k \in \mathbb{N}}$, $\mathcal{C}_{e \to e \to o} = \{=^e\}$, $\mathcal{C}_{(e \to o) \to o} = \{\Pi^e\}$, $\mathcal{P}_e = \{p_e^k\}_{k < m}$, and $\mathcal{P}_{e \to o} = \{p_{e \to o}^k\}_{k < n}$.[3]

In Ex. 2.11 the type e is intended to denote individuals, so that $e \to e$ becomes the type for (unary) functions over individuals. In particular, the symbol Π^e, of type $(e \to o) \to o$, has a fixed intended interpretation as a special second-order predicate assigning true to those unary predicates which are true of every individual (of type e). In general, Π^{α^n} (of type $(\alpha^n \to o) \to o$ for $\alpha \in \tau$) has a fixed interpretation as a special predicate which is true of those predicates/relations of type $\alpha^n \to o$ which are true of all of their arguments (each of type α). We use $\forall x_\alpha . \varphi$ as shorthand for $\Pi^\alpha(\lambda x_\alpha . \varphi)$ and, analogously, $\exists x_\alpha . \varphi$ for $\neg \Pi^\alpha(\lambda x_\alpha . \neg \varphi)$.

Example 2.12 [SOL] An example *F-signature* for second-order logic, with relations, and with two second-order predicates H^1 and H^2, but without any functions is: $\mathcal{S}_{\text{SOL}} = \langle \{\mathcal{C}_{o \to o}, \mathcal{C}_{o \to o \to o}\} \cup \{\mathcal{C}_{(e^n \to o) \to o}\}_{n \in \mathbb{N}} \cup \{\mathcal{C}_{((e \to o)^n \to o) \to o}\}_{n \in \mathbb{N}}$, $\{\mathcal{P}_{(e \to o) \to o}\}\rangle$, with $\mathcal{C}_{o \to o} = \{\neg\}$, $\mathcal{C}_{o \to o \to o} = \{\wedge, \vee, \to\}$, $\mathcal{C}_{(e \to o) \to o} = \{\Pi^e\}$, $\mathcal{C}_{((e \to o) \to o) \to o} = \{\Pi^{(e \to o)}\}$, and $\mathcal{P}_{(e \to o) \to o} = \{H^1, H^2\}$.

Example 2.13 [STT] An example *F-signature* for Church's simple type theory (**STT**; [3]) with countably many parameters (for all types $\alpha \in \tau$) is: $\mathcal{S}_{\text{STT}} = \langle \{\mathcal{C}_o, \mathcal{C}_{o \to o}, \mathcal{C}_{o \to o \to o}\} \cup \{\mathcal{C}_{(\alpha^n \to o) \to o}\}_{\alpha \in \tau, n \in \mathbb{N}}, \{\mathcal{P}_\alpha\}_{\alpha \in \tau}\rangle$, with $\mathcal{C}_o = \{T, F\}$, $\mathcal{C}_{o \to o} = \{\neg\}$, $\mathcal{C}_{o \to o \to o} = \{\wedge, \vee, \to\}$, $\mathcal{C}_{(\alpha \to o) \to o} = \{\Pi^\alpha\}$, and $\mathcal{P}_\alpha = \{p_\alpha^k\}_{k \in \mathbb{N}}$. Syntax and semantics of **STT** is discussed in detail by [4].

We also illustrate the encoding of semantic structures for modal and nonclassical logics. In the sequel, in order to improve readability, σ is used as

---

[3] For convenience, when we have indexed parameters or connectives, we may use their type as an additional label. This way we do not have to define a numbering mechanism for types.

shorthand for type $w\to o$. Thus, symbols of type σ are intended to denote *propositions*, understood as (characteristic functions of) sets of points or 'worlds'.

Example 2.14 [Relational structures] Consider the following *F-signature* for the first-order language of relational structures. $\mathcal{S}_{\text{FORS}} = \langle\{\mathcal{C}_o, \mathcal{C}_{o\to o}, \mathcal{C}_{o\to o\to o}, \mathcal{C}_{\sigma\to o}\}, \{\mathcal{P}_\sigma, \mathcal{P}_{w\to w\to o}\}\rangle$, with $\mathcal{C}_o = \{T, F\}$, $\mathcal{C}_{o\to o} = \{\neg\}$, $\mathcal{C}_{o\to o\to o} = \{\wedge, \vee, \to\}$, $\mathcal{C}_{\sigma\to o} = \{\Pi^w\}$, $\mathcal{P}_\sigma = \{p^k\}_{k\in\mathbb{N}}$, and $\mathcal{P}_{w\to w\to o} = \{R^k\}_{k\in\mathbb{N}}$.

Example 2.15 [Neighborhood structures] Consider the following *F-signature* for a second-order language of neighborhood structures. This example features two kinds of neighborhood functions for monadic and dyadic operators. $\mathcal{S}_{\text{SONS}} = \langle\{\mathcal{C}_{o\to o}, \mathcal{C}_{o\to o\to o}, \mathcal{C}_{\sigma\to o}, \mathcal{C}_{(\sigma\to o)\to o}\}, \{\mathcal{P}_\sigma, \mathcal{P}_{\sigma\to\sigma}, \mathcal{P}_{\sigma\to\sigma\to o}\}\rangle$, with $\mathcal{C}_{o\to o} = \{\neg\}$, $\mathcal{C}_{o\to o\to o} = \{\wedge, \vee, \to\}$, $\mathcal{C}_{\sigma\to o} = \{\Pi^w\}$, $\mathcal{C}_{(\sigma\to o)\to o} = \{\Pi^\sigma\}$, $\mathcal{P}_\sigma = \{p^k\}_{k\in\mathbb{N}}$, $\mathcal{P}_{\sigma\to\sigma} = \{N_1^k\}_{k\in\mathbb{N}}$, and $\mathcal{P}_{\sigma\to\sigma\to o} = \{N_2^k\}_{k\in\mathbb{N}}$.

The previous example deserves some further explanations: In semantical approaches to modal and deontic logics (cf. *minimal* semantics [16] or *neighborhood* semantics [18]), which follow the 'propositions as sets of worlds' paradigm, so-called *neighborhood functions* are usually introduced, in set-theoretical terms, as functions $N : W\to\mathcal{P}(\mathcal{P}(W))$ (where W is the domain set and $\mathcal{P}(W)$ its powerset) that assign to each point/world w a set $N(w)$ of propositions/neighborhoods; this corresponds to the functional type $w\to(w\to o)\to o$. It is evident that N can be associated with a function $N^* : \mathcal{P}(W)\to\mathcal{P}(W)$ that assigns to each proposition φ a proposition $N^*(\varphi)$ corresponding to the set of worlds to which φ gets assigned by N; this corresponds to the functional type $(w\to o)\to(w\to o)$, abbreviated as $\sigma\to\sigma$. Neighborhood functions for sets (often employed in the semantics of dyadic operators and having the form $N : \mathcal{P}(W)\to\mathcal{P}(\mathcal{P}(W)))$ correspond to terms of type $(w\to o)\to(w\to o)\to o$, i.e., $\sigma\to\sigma\to o$. Note that Π^w and Π^σ correspond to quantifiers ranging over worlds and propositions (sets of worlds) respectively.

2.4   Higher-order Languages

Analogous to the propositional case, we define higher-order languages inductively. Again, the grammar remains fixed, so that only the signature changes in each case. We assume a fixed, denumerable set $\mathcal{V} = \{v_\alpha^k\}_{\alpha\in\tau, k\in\mathbb{N}}$ of variables.

Definition 2.16 [F-Language] The (higher-order) *functional language* $L = \mathcal{L}^F(\mathcal{S})$ over F-signature $\mathcal{S} = \langle\mathcal{C}, \mathcal{P}\rangle$ is the smallest set defined inductively as:

(i) $v, p, A \in \mathcal{L}^F(\mathcal{S})$ for every $v \in \mathcal{V}$, $p \in \mathcal{P}_{\alpha\in\tau}$, and $A \in \mathcal{C}_{\alpha\in\tau}$;

(ii) $(A_{\alpha\to\beta} B_\alpha)_\beta \in \mathcal{L}^F(\mathcal{S})$ whenever $A, B \in \mathcal{L}^F(\mathcal{S})$ for all α, β in τ;

(iii) $(\lambda x_\alpha.A_\beta)_{\alpha\to\beta} \in \mathcal{L}^F(\mathcal{S})$ whenever $A \in \mathcal{L}^F(\mathcal{S})$ and $x \in \mathcal{V}$ for all α, β in τ.

The elements of an F-language, i.e., its well-formed formulas, are called *terms*; terms of type o are traditionally called formulas. We define the *grounded*[4] language $\mathcal{L}_{Gr}^F(\mathcal{S})$ over F-signature $\mathcal{S} = \langle\mathcal{C}, \mathcal{P}\rangle$ as the language over

---

[4] For want of a better word, we call terms 'grounded' when they are 'parameter-free'. Note that this may not coincide with other uses of 'grounded' in the literature.

$\mathcal{S}^{Gr} = \langle \mathcal{C}, \emptyset \rangle$. A term is called *closed* if it does not contain any free variables. [5] We define the *language of closed terms* of a language $\mathcal{L}$ $(= \mathcal{L}^F(\mathcal{S}))$ as the subset of $\mathcal{L}$ consisting of all of its closed terms; this language is noted $Closed(\mathcal{L})$.

Example 2.17 The F-signature presented in Ex. 2.10 induces a language $\mathcal{L}^F(\mathcal{S}_{\text{CPL-F}})$. This language has the same expressivity as the P-language $\mathcal{L}^P(\mathcal{S}_{\text{CPL}})$ in Ex. 2.2 if we neglect λ-abstraction (last item in Def. 2.16).

Example 2.18 The F-signature presented in Ex. 2.13 induces a language $\mathcal{L}^F(\mathcal{S}_{\text{STT}})$ for Church's simple theory of types (**STT**); cf. [3].

Example 2.19 The F-signature in Ex. 2.11 induces a language $\mathcal{L}^F(\mathcal{S}_{\text{FOL}})$, corresponding to *extended first-order logic* [10], an **STT**-fragment with equality and quantification for objects of base type e, which retains λ-abstraction and higher-order variables. (We obtain classical FOL by neglecting the latter two.)

Example 2.20 The F-signature presented in Ex. 2.14 (Ex. 2.15) induces a first- (second-) order language $\mathcal{L}^F(\mathcal{S}_{\text{FORS}})$ $(\mathcal{L}^F(\mathcal{S}_{\text{SONS}}))$ that can be used to define connectives and formulate semantic conditions for (non-)normal modal logics in the style of Kripke (neighborhood [18]) semantics.

3   Shallow Embeddings as Derived Signatures

A signature is thus composed of (type-indexed) sets of symbols, divided into connectives $\mathcal{C}$ and parameters $\mathcal{P}$. Notice that these symbols adopt a double role as both atomic building blocks and terms (well-formed formulas) of a language. We can naturally ask whether terms, in general, can act as atomic building blocks in the construction of languages; or more specifically, whether terms, as symbols, can also adopt the role of connectives in signatures. We give this question a positive answer by introducing the notion of *derived signatures*.

3.1   Derived Signatures

Informally, derived signatures arise when we allow *closed* terms to play the role of logical connectives. They are called *derived* because they rely on an already existing language, itself induced by a different, 'primitive' signature. In such cases we say that signature $\mathcal{S}^D$ has been *derived* from signature $\mathcal{S}$ and introduce the relation $derived(\mathcal{S}^D, \mathcal{S})$ to indicate this. We differentiate between *rigidly* and *flexibly* derived signatures. We define the first recursively. We introduce the predicate $rigid(\mathcal{S})$ to indicate that $\mathcal{S}$ is either primitive or rigidly derived.

Definition 3.1 [Rigidly Derived Signature] A signature $\mathcal{S}^D = \langle \mathcal{C}^D, \mathcal{P}^D \rangle$ is said to be *rigidly derived* from signature $\mathcal{S} = \langle \mathcal{C}, \mathcal{P} \rangle$ provided that $rigid(\mathcal{S})$ and, for each type $\alpha \in \tau$, we have that $\mathcal{P}^D_\alpha \subseteq \mathcal{P}_\alpha$ and each connective $c \in \mathcal{C}^D_\alpha$ belongs to $Closed(\mathcal{L}^F_{Gr}(\mathcal{S}))$.

Hence, the connectives of a rigidly derived signature $\mathcal{S}^D$ are closed terms of the grounded language over $\mathcal{S}$ and its parameters are simply a subset of those

---

[5] Free variables are those which appear either outside any λ-expression, or unbound inside some λ-expression; cf. [3] for a detailed exposition.

of $\mathcal{S}$, provided that $\mathcal{S}$ is itself a rigid signature. Notice that the connectives so generated will get the same interpretation in all models; in other words, they are *rigidly* interpreted. In this respect, rigidly derived signatures behave in fact like primitive ones, in contrast to flexibly derived signatures.

Definition 3.2 [Flexibly Derived Signature] A signature $\mathcal{S}^D = \langle \mathcal{C}^D, \mathcal{P}^D \rangle$ is said to be *flexibly derived* from signature $\mathcal{S} = \langle \mathcal{C}, \mathcal{P} \rangle$ if, for each type $\alpha \in \tau$, we have that $\mathcal{P}_\alpha^D \subseteq \mathcal{P}_\alpha$ and each connective $c \in \mathcal{C}_\alpha^D$ belongs to $Closed(\mathcal{L}^F(\mathcal{S}))$.

Thus, the connectives of a flexibly derived signature $\mathcal{S}^D$ are closed terms of the language over $\mathcal{S}$ (without further restrictions). Note that, since parameters are also closed terms of the language $\mathcal{L}^F(\mathcal{S})$, the elements of $\mathcal{P}^D$ can also be considered as elements of $\mathcal{C}^D$. Also notice that these 'flexible' connectives, in contrast to those of a primitive or a rigidly derived signature, may get different interpretations in different models.

Example 3.3 [Relational and neighborhood signatures as rigidly derived] Note that $\mathcal{S}_{\mathrm{FORS}}$ and $\mathcal{S}_{\mathrm{SONS}}$ (introduced in Ex. 2.14 and 2.15 for relational and neighborhood structures respectively) are proper subsets of the signature $\mathcal{S}_{\mathrm{STT}}$. Hence $\mathcal{L}^F(\mathcal{S}_{\mathrm{FORS}})$ and $\mathcal{L}^F(\mathcal{S}_{\mathrm{SONS}})$ are proper fragments of $\mathcal{L}^F(\mathcal{S}_{\mathrm{STT}})$.

We provide examples illustrating how some non-classical logics, relevant to normative reasoning, can be syntactically (and indirectly semantically) characterized as fragments of a higher-order language, e.g. $\mathcal{L}^F(\mathcal{S}_{\mathrm{STT}})$. We recall that σ is employed as shorthand for the type $w{\to}o$, which can be understood as the type of characteristic functions associated with sets of worlds (or propositions, cf. 'truth-sets'). We introduce the following convenient abbreviations; cf. [7]:

Definition 3.4 [(Type-lifted) Boolean connectives]

$\dot{\wedge} := \lambda\varphi.\lambda\psi.\lambda w.(\varphi\ w) \wedge (\psi\ w)$ $\dot{\to} := \lambda\varphi.\lambda\psi.\lambda w.(\varphi\ w) \to (\psi\ w)$

$\dot{\vee} := \lambda\varphi.\lambda\psi.\lambda w.(\varphi\ w) \vee (\psi\ w)$ $\dot{\neg} := \lambda\varphi.\lambda w.\neg(\varphi\ w)$

Example 3.5 [Rigidly derived signature for S5U] We add the following abbreviation to those in Def. 3.4: $\dot{\Box}^u := \lambda\varphi.\lambda w.\forall v.(\varphi\ v)$. A signature for modal logic **S5U** (with universal modality) is given by $\mathcal{S}_{\mathrm{S5U}} = \langle\{\{\dot{\neg}, \dot{\Box}^u\}_{\sigma\to\sigma}, \{\dot{\wedge}, \dot{\vee}, \dot{\to}\}_{\sigma\to\sigma\to\sigma}\}, \{\{p^k\}_\sigma^{k\in\mathbb{N}}\}\rangle$, which has been *rigidly* derived from the signature $\mathcal{S}_{\mathrm{FORS}}$ for relational structures introduced in Ex. 2.14.

In the remainder each R^i represents an arbitrary relation. Similarly N_1^i and N_2^i represent neighborhood functions for points and sets respectively.

Example 3.6 [Flexibly derived signature for a normal modal logic] We set as abbreviations: $\dot{\Box}^a := \lambda\varphi.\lambda w.\forall v.(R^1\ w)\ v \to (\varphi\ v)$, $\dot{\Box}^p := \lambda\varphi.\lambda w.\forall v.(R^2\ w)\ v \to (\varphi\ v)$, $\Diamond^a := \lambda\varphi.\dot{\neg}\ \dot{\Box}^a\ \dot{\neg}\varphi$, and $\Diamond^p := \lambda\varphi.\dot{\neg}\ \dot{\Box}^p\ \dot{\neg}\varphi$. A signature for the (bimodal) normal modal logic (extending **K**) is given by $\mathcal{S}_{\mathrm{BMLK}} = \langle\{\{\dot{\neg}, \dot{\Box}^a, \Diamond^a, \dot{\Box}^p, \Diamond^p\}_{\sigma\to\sigma}, \{\dot{\wedge}, \dot{\vee}, \dot{\to}\}_{\sigma\to\sigma\to\sigma}\}, \{\{p^k\}_\sigma^{k\in\mathbb{N}}\}\rangle$, which is *flexibly* derived from the signature for relational structures $\mathcal{S}_{\mathrm{FORS}}$ introduced in Ex. 2.14. Extensions of **K** are obtained by correspondingly restricting R^1 and R^2.

Example 3.7 [Flexibly derived signature for a non-normal modal logic] We set abbreviations: $\dot{O}^d := \lambda\psi.\lambda\varphi.\lambda w.(N_2^1\ \varphi)\ \psi$, $\dot{O}^a := \lambda\varphi.\lambda w.(N_2^1\ (R^1\ w))\ \varphi$, and $\dot{O}^p := \lambda\varphi.\lambda w.(N_2^1 \ (R^2 \ w)) \ \varphi$. Consider the following signature for a non-normal modal logic featuring two monadic and one dyadic operator: $\mathcal{S}_{\mathrm{DML}} = \langle\{\{\neg, \dot{O}^a, \dot{O}^b\}_{\sigma\to\sigma}, \{\wedge, \vee, \to, \dot{O}^d\}_{\sigma\to\sigma\to\sigma}\}, \{\{p^k\}_\sigma^{k\in\mathbb{N}}\}\rangle$, which has been *flexibly* derived from the signature $\mathcal{S}_{\mathrm{FORS}} \cup \mathcal{S}_{\mathrm{SONS}}$.

As an example application in normative reasoning, observe that the signature for the language of the *dyadic deontic logic* (**DDL**) by Carmo & Jones [11] corresponds (up to presentation) to the (component-wise) union of the three signatures introduced in the examples above: $\mathcal{S}_{\mathrm{DDL}} = \mathcal{S}_{\mathrm{S5U}} \cup \mathcal{S}_{\mathrm{BMLK}} \cup \mathcal{S}_{\mathrm{DML}}$. Hence $\mathcal{S}_{\mathrm{DDL}}$ is flexibly derived from the 'primitive' signature $\mathcal{S}_{\mathrm{STT}}$, and thus $\mathcal{L}^F(\mathcal{S}_{\mathrm{DDL}})$ is a (proper) fragment of $\mathcal{L}^F(\mathcal{S}_{\mathrm{STT}})$. The semantic conditions imposed for **DDL**-frames (e.g. reflexivity, resp. seriality for accessibility relations and the closure conditions for the neighborhood function) translate in our approach to formulas of the host language $\mathcal{L}^F(\mathcal{S}_{\mathrm{STT}})$. In the spirit of previous work on the shallow semantical embeddings (SSE) of object logics in higher-order logic, we may speak in the present case of a SSE of the object logic **DDL** into the meta-logic **STT** (cf. the encoding of **DDL** in Isabelle/HOL in [5]).

In order to generalize, and formally define, the notions discussed in the above example, some remarks on terminology are in order. We conceive of a logic **L** as a formal language $\mathcal{L}$, together with a consequence relation $\vdash_L \subset \mathcal{P}(\mathcal{L}) \times \mathcal{L}$, where the latter can be defined model-theoretically or proof-theoretically. We write $\mathbf{L}_{(i)}$ to refer to the logic based upon the language $\mathcal{L}_{(i)}$.

Definition 3.8 [SSEs as derived F-signatures] Let $\mathcal{S}^O$ be a derived 'object' signature, such that $derived(\mathcal{S}^O, \mathcal{S}^H)$ for some 'host' F-signature $\mathcal{S}^H$. Furthermore, let us assume an (informal) interpretation of the connectives of $\mathcal{S}^O$ as corresponding to the connectives of some 'object' logic $\mathbf{L}^O$. Moreover, let us consider a (higher-order) logic $\mathbf{L}^H$ based upon the language $\mathcal{L}^F(\mathcal{S}^H)$ together with a set of formulas $\Gamma \subset \mathcal{L}^F(\mathcal{S}^H)$ interpreted as 'semantic conditions'. We say that $\mathcal{S}^O$ is a *shallow semantical embedding* (SSE) for the 'object' logic $\mathbf{L}^O$ into the 'meta-logic' $\mathbf{L}^H$ after defining a special predicate $vld(\cdot)$ in $\mathcal{L}^F(\mathcal{S}^H)$, such that, for any $\varphi \in \mathcal{L}^F(\mathcal{S}^O)$, $\Gamma \vdash_{\mathbf{L}^H} vld(\varphi)$ iff $\vdash_{\mathbf{L}^O} \varphi$.

From the above definition it follows that $\mathcal{L}^F(\mathcal{S}^O)$ is a fragment of $\mathcal{L}^F(\mathcal{S}^H)$. Note also that the condition of *faithfulness* of the SSE has been integrated in the definition. This last condition can be weakened for particular purposes.

Example 3.9 [SSE of modal logics into STT] We obtain SSEs from derived 'modal' signatures (e.g. in Ex. 3.5–3.7) by defining the $\mathcal{L}^F(\mathcal{S}_{STT})$ predicate $vld := \lambda\varphi.(\Pi^w \ \varphi)$ and appropriately encoding the corresponding semantic conditions (e.g. via Sahlqvist correspondence).

The logic combination [6] of a pair $\mathbf{L}_1$, $\mathbf{L}_2$ (resp. an i-indexed set $\mathbf{L}_i$) of logics is termed $\mathbf{L}_1 \oplus \mathbf{L}_2$ (resp. $\bigoplus \mathbf{L}_i$). Recall from Ex. 3.7 and its subsequent discussion, that a SSE for the **DDL** [11] corresponds to the signature $\mathcal{S}_{\mathrm{DDL}} = \mathcal{S}_{\mathrm{S5U}} \cup \mathcal{S}_{\mathrm{BMLK}} \cup \mathcal{S}_{\mathrm{DML}}$. We can indeed define a combination mechanism for

---

[6] There exist several logic combination mechanisms in the literature; cf. [12]

SSEs of logics such that it corresponds to the union of their (derived) signatures. Their corresponding (meta-logical) semantic conditions can indeed be grouped together (as long as they are consistent). As a further example, we can conceive of a paraconsistent dyadic deontic logic, say **PDDL**, obtained as **DDL⊕P** for some Logic of Formal Inconsistency (LFI) [7] **P** such that $\mathcal{S}_{\text{PDDL}} = \mathcal{S}_{\text{DDL}} \cup \mathcal{S}_{\text{LFI}}$.

Example 3.10 [SSE for LFIs] We set abbreviations: $\dot{\neg}^p := \lambda\varphi.\, \varphi \dot{\rightarrow} (N_1^1\,\varphi)$, and $\dot{\circ} := \lambda\varphi.\, \dot{\neg}(\varphi \dot{\wedge} (N_1^1\,\varphi)) \dot{\wedge} (N_1^2\,\varphi)$. A SSE for LFIs (with replacement and based on a neighborhood semantics [13]) can employ the following signature: $\mathcal{S}_{\text{LFI}} = \langle\{\{\dot{\neg}^p, \dot{\circ}\}_{\sigma\to\sigma}, \{\dot{\wedge}, \dot{\vee}, \dot{\rightarrow}\}_{\sigma\to\sigma\to\sigma}\}, \{\{p^k\}_\sigma^{k\in\mathbb{N}}\}\rangle$, which is *flexibly* derived from the signature $\mathcal{S}_{\text{SONS}}$ in Ex. 2.15. Different logics in this class of LFIs are obtained by suitably restricting the neighborhood functions N_1^1 and N_2^1 [13].

Note that in flexibly derived signatures logical connectives may get different interpretations in different models, since connectives are articulated by employing parameters such as accessibility relations or neighborhood functions (R_i and N_i in the examples above) that do not have a fixed interpretation. While this phenomenon is characteristic of modal logic, our logico-pluralist approach readily exploits (and generalizes) it to non-classical logics. This allows us, for instance, to consider the logic of formalization as an additional degree of freedom in the process of logical analysis of argumentative discourse [17], where we can 'switch' between object logics, based upon flexibly derived signatures, by adding/removing meta-logical axioms in the host logic (intended as object-logical semantic conditions); thus blurring the distinction between logical and extralogical (resp. syncategorematic and categorematic) expressions.

4   Encoding Formal Argumentation

We propose a logico-pluralist characterization for arguments and their dialectical relations in line with the SSE approach as discussed in the previous sections.

Definition 4.1 An $\mathcal{L}$-*argument* (or *L-argument* where L is any $\mathcal{L}$-based logic) is a pair $\langle\Gamma, \varphi\rangle$, where $\Gamma \cup \{\varphi\}$ is a set of $\mathcal{L}$-formulas. The Γ are termed *premises*, and φ is termed *conclusion* (of the argument). Let A be an $\mathcal{L}$-argument. We define the functions *Premises(A)* and *Conclusion(A)*, which return Γ and φ respectively. Moreover, A is said to be *L-deductive* if $\Gamma \vdash_L \varphi$, and *L-(in)consistent* if *Premises(A)* is logically (in)consistent according to L.

As an illustration, we provide a logico-pluralist definition of joint support.

Definition 4.2 [Support] The i-indexed set of L_i-arguments A_i *supports* L_2-argument B if the argument $\langle\bigcup Conclusion(A_i), \psi\rangle$, with $\psi \in Premises(B)$, is L-deductive for the logic combination $L = \bigoplus L_i \oplus L_2$.

---

[7] The class LFI of paraconsistent logics was introduced in [15]. They feature a non-explosive negation ¬, as well as a (primitive or derived) consistency connective ∘ which allows to recover the law of explosion in a controlled way [14]. It has been shown recently that some logics in the hierarchy of LFIs (starting with the minimal logic *mbC*) can be enriched with replacement, and thus given algebraic and neighborhood semantics [13].

Similarly to well-known approaches towards structured argumentation (cf. [8]) different kinds of *attack* relations between arguments can be introduced in a logico-pluralist fashion. Observe that the given definitions have the benefit of not featuring negation. This allows us to apply them to any (non-classical) logics L_i irrespective of the properties satisfied by their negation operator(s); this includes e.g. the paraconsistent LFIs in Ex. 3.10, which provide their own particular mechanisms for defining logical (in)consistency (cf. [14] for a discussion). Moreover, we can take special measures in case the involved arguments are (or not) deductive or consistent. Note also that these definitions can be seamlessly extended to two (or more) attacking arguments.

Definition 4.3 [Undermine] L_1-argument A *undermines* L_2-argument B if *Conclusion*$(A) \cup$ *Premises*(A) is $L_1 \oplus L_2$-inconsistent.

Definition 4.4 [Rebuttal] L_1-argument A *rebuts* L_2-argument B if *Conclusion*$(A) \cup$ *Conclusion*(B) is $L_1 \oplus L_2$-inconsistent.

Definition 4.5 [Deductive Undercut] L_1-argument A *undercuts* L_2-argument B if $\vdash_{L_1}$ *Conclusion*(A) implies (metalogically) that B is not L_2-deductive.

Arguably, the last definition above can be seen as a special kind of undercut. It can be given an informal reading, namely, that if the conclusion of argument A holds, then the argument B is not *valid*.

5   Conclusion and Further Work

As a first contribution, this article introduces a conceptual framework, together with illustrative examples, enabling an improved 'syntax-oriented' (and thus 'user-oriented') characterization and analysis of the *shallow semantical embeddings* (SSE) technique. We expect that this framework will leverage communication and better support the development of more concise SSEs of logics and logic combinations. In particular, faithfulness proofs, which have been very technical and verbose so far, will benefit from being stated (and even carried out) much more concisely. This represents an important step towards a systematic method for encoding logics (modal, deontic, paraconsistent, etc.) in higher-order logic, a pillar stone of the LogiKEy framework and methodology for designing normative theories in ethical and legal reasoning [6].

Recent work [20] shows that the expressivity of higher-order logic indeed allows us to encode several notions of abstract argumentation frameworks [1], and to mechanize reasoning with them, e.g., by harnessing *Isabelle/HOL*'s integrated reasoning tools [9] to generate arguments' extensions and labellings, and to carry out meta-theoretical investigations. As a second main contribution, the present work connects to those efforts by considering the instantiation of abstract arguments and their dialectical relations as structured entities, in a logico-pluralist spirit. This is useful for prototyping tasks involving reasoning with (small) argument networks at the abstract and structural level in an integrated fashion. Ongoing and future work is geared towards providing a scalable implementation by integrating specialist argumentation solvers and tools.

References

[1] Baroni, P., M. Caminada and M. Giacomin, *An introduction to argumentation semantics*, Knowledge Engineering Review **26** (2011), pp. 365–410.

[2] Benzmüller, C., *Universal (meta-)logical reasoning: Recent successes*, Science of Computer Programming **172** (2019), pp. 48–62.

[3] Benzmüller, C. and P. Andrews, *Church's Type Theory*, in: E. N. Zalta, editor, *The Stanford Encyclopedia of Philosophy*, Metaphysics Research Lab, Stanford University, 2019, summer 2019 edition .

[4] Benzmüller, C., C. Brown and M. Kohlhase, *Higher-order semantics and extensionality*, Journal of Symbolic Logic **69** (2004), pp. 1027–1088.

[5] Benzmüller, C., A. Farjami and X. Parent, *Dyadic deontic logic in hol: Faithful embedding and meta-theoretical experiments*, in: S. Rahman, M. Armgardt and H. C. N. Kvernenes, editors, *New Developments in Legal Reasoning and Logic: From Ancient Law to Modern Legal Systems*, Springer International Publishing, Cham, 2022 pp. 353–377.

[6] Benzmüller, C., X. Parent and L. van der Torre, *Designing normative theories for ethical and legal reasoning: LogiKEy framework, methodology, and tool support*, Artificial Intelligence **287** (2020), p. 103348.

[7] Benzmüller, C. and L. C. Paulson, *Quantified multimodal logics in simple type theory*, Logica Universalis (Special Issue on Multimodal Logics) **7** (2013), pp. 7–20.

[8] Besnard, P. and A. Hunter, *Constructing argument graphs with deductive arguments: a tutorial*, Argument & Computation **5** (2014), pp. 5–30.

[9] Blanchette, J. C., C. Kaliszyk, L. C. Paulson and J. Urban, *Hammering towards QED*, Journal of Formalized Reasoning **9** (2016), pp. 101–148.

[10] Brown, C. E. and G. Smolka, *Extended first-order logic*, in: *International Conference on Theorem Proving in Higher Order Logics*, Springer, 2009, pp. 164–179.

[11] Carmo, J. and A. J. Jones, *Deontic logic and contrary-to-duties*, in: *Handbook of philosophical logic*, Springer, 2002 pp. 265–343.

[12] Carnielli, W. and M. E. Coniglio, *Combining Logics*, in: E. N. Zalta, editor, *The Stanford Encyclopedia of Philosophy*, Metaphysics Research Lab, Stanford University, 2020, Fall 2020 edition .

[13] Carnielli, W., M. E. Coniglio and D. Fuenmayor, *Logics of formal inconsistency enriched with replacement: An algebraic and modal account*, The Review of Symbolic Logic (2021), p. 1–36, online first.

[14] Carnielli, W. A., M. E. Coniglio and A. Rodrigues, *Recovery operators, paraconsistency and duality*, Logic Journal of the IGPL **28** (2020), pp. 624–656.

[15] Carnielli, W. A. and J. Marcos, *A taxonomy of c-systems*, in: *Paraconsistency*, CRC Press, 2002 pp. 24–117.

[16] Chellas, B. F., "Modal logic: an introduction," Cambridge university press, 1980.

[17] Fuenmayor, D. and C. Benzmüller, *A computational-hermeneutic approach for conceptual explicitation*, in: A. Nepomuceno, L. Magnani, F. Salguero, C. Bares and M. Fontaine, editors, *Model-Based Reasoning in Science and Technology. Inferential Models for Logic, Language, Cognition and Computation*, SAPERE **49**, Springer, 2019 pp. 441–469.

[18] Pacuit, E., "Neighborhood semantics for modal logic," Springer, 2017.

[19] Steen, A. and C. Benzmüller, *Sweet SIXTEEN: Automation via embedding into classical higher-order logic*, Logic and Logical Philosophy **25** (2016), pp. 535–554.

[20] Steen, A. and D. Fuenmayor, *A formalisation of abstract argumentation in higher-order logic*, Journal of Logic and Computation (2022), accepted for publication. Pre-print available at https://arxiv.org/abs/2110.09174.

New Axiomatization of Lewis' Conditional Logics

Xuefeng Wen [1]

Sun Yat-sen University

Abstract

We shows that the popular axiomatic systems proposed by Nute for Lewis' conditional logics are not equivalent to Lewis' original systems. In particular, the axiom CA which is derivable in Lewis' systems is not derivable in Nute's systems. Then we propose a new set of axiomatizations for Lewis' conditional logics, without using CSO, or RCEA, or the rule of interchange of logical equivalents. Instead, the new axiomatizations adopt two axioms which correspond to cautious monotonicity and cautious cut in nonmonotonic logics, respectively. Finally, we gives a simple resolution to a puzzle about the controversial axiom of simplification of disjunctive antecedents, using a long neglected axiom in one of Lewis' systems for conditional logics.

Keywords: conditional logic, axiomatization, simplification of disjunctive antecedents, nonmonotonic logic.

1 Introduction

Lewis proposed two conditional logics, denoted by **V** and **VC**, respectively. Each of them has three different axiomatizations in the literature. Two were proposed by Lewis himself, one in [7], where **V** and **VC** were named **C0** and **C1**, respectively, the other in [9]. A third formulation was offered by Nute [14,16,17]. Lewis' formulations have less but some cumbersome axioms. Nute's formulations have more but neater axioms, making them easier to compare with other systems. Thus, Nute's axiomatizations are more popular in the literature now. When referring to Lewis' conditional logics, often are Nute's axiomatizations presented, for instance in [2] and [19]. [2] We will show in this paper, however, that Nute's systems are not equivalent to Lewis' original ones. In particular, the axiom CA derivable from Lewis' systems is not derivable from Nute's systems. By replacing MOD with CA in Nute's systems, the defects can be amended.

---

[1] wxflogic@gmail.com. This research was supported by the 2021 Humanities and Social Science General Program sponsored by the Ministry of Education of China (Grant No. 21YJA72040001). I thank one referee for correcting several minor mistakes.

[2] In [2], the author wrote: "...it is useful to see first that the system VC can be axiomatized via the axioms ID, MP, MOD, CSO, CV and CS with RCEC and RCK as rules of inference."

Both Lewis' systems in [7] and Nute's systems contain the axiom CSO, which says that bi-conditionally implied propositions can be interchanged with each other for antecedents. From CSO together with RCE (namely a conditional from φ to ψ can be derived if φ entails ψ), the rule of interchange of logical equivalents for antecedents (RCEA, henceforth) can be derived. Instead of CSO, Lewis' systems in [9] contain the rule of interchange of logical equivalents (RE, henceforth). We will propose some new axiomatizations for Lewis' logics. They contain neither CSO, nor RCEA or RE, and hence may shed light on nonclassical conditional logics, where these axiom and rules are invalidated. The new systems we propose indicate that it is hard to abandon these axiom and rules in conditional logics, since they can be recovered from other intuitive axioms.

Finally, we will show that an axiom in one of Lewis' systems can be used to solve a puzzle triggered by the controversial axiom of simplification of disjunctive antecedents (SDA, henceforth), which is intuitively valid but trivializes conditional implication to strict implication if added to any conditional logic with RCEA.

2   Preliminaries

For reference, we list all related axioms and rules for conditional logics in this paper as follows:

(PC)   All tautologies and derivable rules in classical logic

(ID) $\varphi > \varphi$

(CM) $(\varphi > \psi \wedge \chi) \rightarrow (\varphi > \psi) \wedge (\varphi > \chi)$

(CC) $(\varphi > \psi) \wedge (\varphi > \chi) \rightarrow (\varphi > \psi \wedge \chi)$

(CV) $(\varphi > \chi) \wedge \neg(\varphi > \neg\psi) \rightarrow (\varphi \wedge \psi > \chi)$

(CA) $(\varphi > \chi) \wedge (\psi > \chi) \rightarrow (\varphi \vee \psi > \chi)$

(AC) $(\varphi > \psi) \wedge (\varphi > \chi) \rightarrow (\varphi \wedge \psi > \chi)$

(RT) $(\varphi > \psi) \wedge (\psi \wedge \varphi > \chi) \rightarrow (\varphi > \chi)$

(CSO) $(\varphi > \psi) \wedge (\psi > \varphi) \rightarrow ((\varphi > \chi) \leftrightarrow (\psi > \chi))$

(MOD) $(\varphi > \neg\varphi) \rightarrow (\psi > \neg\varphi)$

(DAE) $(\varphi \vee \psi > \varphi) \vee (\varphi \vee \psi > \psi) \vee ((\varphi \vee \psi > \chi) \leftrightarrow (\varphi > \chi) \wedge (\psi > \chi))$

(PIE) $(\varphi > \neg\psi) \vee ((\varphi \wedge \psi > \chi) \leftrightarrow (\varphi > (\psi \rightarrow \chi)))$

(CMP) $(\varphi > \psi) \rightarrow (\varphi \rightarrow \psi)$

(CS) $\varphi \wedge \psi \rightarrow (\varphi > \psi)$

(SDA) $(\varphi \vee \psi > \chi) \rightarrow (\varphi > \chi) \wedge (\psi > \chi)$

(RCM) $\dfrac{\varphi \rightarrow \psi}{(\chi > \varphi) \rightarrow (\chi > \psi)}$

(RCE) $\dfrac{\varphi \rightarrow \psi}{\varphi > \psi}$

(RCN) $$\dfrac{\psi}{\varphi > \psi}$$

(RCK) $$\dfrac{\psi_1 \wedge \ldots \wedge \psi_n \to \psi}{(\varphi > \psi_1) \wedge \ldots \wedge (\varphi > \psi_n) \to (\varphi > \psi)} \quad (n \geq 0)$$

(RCEA) $$\dfrac{\varphi \leftrightarrow \psi}{(\varphi > \chi) \leftrightarrow (\psi > \chi)}$$

(RCEC) $$\dfrac{\varphi \leftrightarrow \psi}{(\chi > \varphi) \leftrightarrow (\chi > \psi)}$$

(RE) $$\dfrac{\psi \leftrightarrow \psi'}{\varphi \leftrightarrow \varphi[\psi/\psi']}$$

All the axioms and rules above had been discussed in the literature (e.g. [9,14,16]) before. Note that we slightly reformulate the axiom MOD here. The standard formulation of MOD in the literature (including Lewis' works) is

MOD' $(\neg\varphi > \varphi) \to (\psi > \varphi).$

The reason why we reformulate it is that it is this reformulation rather than the standard one that corresponds directly to the associated model condition of worlds selection functions, normally formulated in the literature as follows:

(mod) $f(w, \varphi) = \emptyset \implies f(w, \psi) \cap [\varphi] = \emptyset,$

where $[\psi]$ denotes the truth set of ψ, and f is the selection function, associating with a possible world w and a sentence φ a set of φ- worlds that are closest to w. Rather, the standard formulation MOD' corresponds to the following condition instead:

(mod') $f(w, \neg\varphi) = \emptyset \implies f(w, \psi) \cap [\neg\varphi] = \emptyset.$

Of course, if the rules RCEA and RCEC, or the rule RE is available, the difference between the two formulations is immaterial. But if one works on conditional logics without such rules admissible, the two formulations might turn out to be very different. This is related to my second reason for choosing the reformulation. In a proof of the derivation of CSO from MOD' and PIE below, we find if the reformulation MOD is used then the rule RCEA or RE is dispensable; otherwise, such rules are required for the derivation.

3   Amendments of Nute's Axiomatizations

Nute's axiomatization for **V** and **VC** are as follows [3]

$$\mathbf{Vn} = \langle \text{PC}, \text{ID}, \text{CM}, \text{CC}, \text{CV}, \text{MOD}', \text{CSO}; \text{RCEC} \rangle$$
$$\mathbf{VCn} = \langle \text{PC}, \text{ID}, \text{CM}, \text{CC}, \text{CV}, \text{MOD}', \text{CSO}, \text{CMP}, \text{CS}; \text{RCEC} \rangle.$$

---

[3] Nute's original axiomatization used the rule RCK instead of the axioms CM and CC. But to reduce inference rules to the minimum, we prefer to use these two axioms instead of the rule RCK. It can be easily shown that they are equivalent as long as RCEC is provided.

We will show that CA is not derivable in neither of these systems. Since **VCn** is the stronger one, it suffices to prove that CA is not derivable in **VCn**.

Proposition 3.1 $\nvdash_{\textbf{VCn}}$ CA.

Proof. Let $U = \{0,1,2,3\}$, $A = \{1,2\}$, and $B = \{1,3\}$. Define $g : U \times \wp(U) \to \wp(U)$ as follows:

$$g(i, X) = \begin{cases} \{1\} & \text{if } X = A \text{ and } i = 0 \\ \{i\} & \text{if } i \in X \\ X & \text{otherwise} \end{cases}$$

Now we verify that g satisfies the following conditions: for all $i \in U$ and $X, Y \in \wp(U)$

(id) $g(i, X) \subseteq X$

(mod) $g(i, X) = \emptyset \Longrightarrow g(i, Y) \cap X = \emptyset$

(cv) $g(i, X) \cap Y \neq \emptyset \Longrightarrow g(i, X \cap Y) \subseteq g(i, X)$

(cso) $g(i, X) \subseteq Y$ and $g(i, Y) \subseteq X \Longrightarrow g(i, X) = g(i, Y)$

(cent) $i \in X \Longrightarrow g(i, X) = \{i\}$

(id) and (cent) are obvious. (mod) holds since $g(i, X) = \emptyset$ iff $X = \emptyset$. It remains to verify (cv) and (cso). For (cv), suppose $g(i, X) \cap Y \neq \emptyset$. Consider the following cases:

(1) $X = A$ and $i = 0$. Then $g(i, X) = \{1\}$. Since $g(i, X) \cap Y \neq \emptyset$, we have $1 \in Y$. Hence $X \cap Y = X$ or $X \cap Y = \{1\}$. In both cases, we have $g(i, X \cap Y) = g(i, X)$.

(2) $i \in X$. Then $g(i, X) = \{i\}$. Since $g(i, X) \cap Y \neq \emptyset$, we have $i \in Y$. Then $i \in X \cap Y$. Hence $g(i, X \cap Y) = \{i\} = g(i, X)$.

(3) $X \neq A$ or $i \neq 0$, and $i \notin X$. Then $g(i, X) = X$. Since $i \notin X$, we have $i \notin X \cap Y$. Then either $g(i, X \cap Y) = \{1\}$ or $g(i, X \cap Y) = X \cap Y$. If $g(i, X \cap Y) = X \cap Y$, we have $g(i, X \cap Y) \subseteq X = g(i, X)$. If $g(i, X \cap Y) \neq X \cap Y$ and $g(i, X \cap Y) = \{1\}$, by the definition of g, we have $X \cap Y = A$. Hence $1 \in X$ and $g(i, X \cap Y) \subseteq g(i, X)$. .

For (cso), suppose $g(i, X) \subseteq Y$ and $g(i, Y) \subseteq X$. Consider the following cases:

(1) $X = A$ and $i = 0$. Then $g(i, X) = \{1\}$. Since $g(i, X) \subseteq Y$, we have $1 \in Y$. Since $g(i, Y) \subseteq X$ and $i \notin X$, we have $Y = A$ or $g(i, Y) = Y \subseteq X$. In the former case, we have $g(i, X) = g(i, Y)$. In the latter case, we have $Y = \{1\}$, and hence $g(i, Y) = \{1\} = g(i, X)$.

(2) $i \in X$. Then $g(i, X) = \{i\}$. Since $g(i, X) \subseteq Y$, we have $i \in Y$. Hence $g(i, Y) = \{i\} = g(i, X)$.

(3) $X \neq A$ or $i \neq 0$, and $i \notin X$. Then $g(i, X) = X$. Since $g(i, X) \subseteq Y$, we have $X \subseteq Y$. If $Y = A$ and $i = 0$, then $g(i, Y) = \{1\}$. By $g(i, Y) \subseteq X$, we have $1 \in X$. Then by $X \subseteq Y = A$, we have $X = \{1\}$ or $X = Y$.

In both cases we have $g(i, X) = g(i, Y)$. If $i \in Y$, then $g(i, Y) = \{i\}$. Since $g(i, Y) \subseteq X$, we have $i \in X$, contradicting that $i \notin X$. In other cases, we have $g(i, Y) = Y$. Since $g(i, Y) \subseteq X$, we have $Y \subseteq X$. Hence $g(i, X) = g(i, Y)$.

Given a model $\mathfrak{M} = (W, f, V)$, the truth set of φ in $\mathfrak{M}$, denoted $[\varphi]^{\mathfrak{M}}$, is inductively defined as follows:

- $[p]^{\mathfrak{M}} = V(p)$ for $p \in PV$
- $[\neg\varphi]^{\mathfrak{M}} = W - [\varphi]^{\mathfrak{M}}$
- $[\varphi \wedge \psi]^{\mathfrak{M}} = [\varphi]^{\mathfrak{M}} \cap [\psi]^{\mathfrak{M}}$
- $[\varphi > \psi]^{\mathfrak{M}} = \{w \in W \mid f(w, [\varphi]^{\mathfrak{M}}) \subseteq [\psi]^{\mathfrak{M}}\}$

We say that φ is valid in $\mathfrak{F} = (W, f)$ if for all models $\mathfrak{M}$ based on $\mathfrak{F}$, $[\varphi]^{\mathfrak{M}} = W$. Let $\mathfrak{G} = (U, g)$. By the frame conditions that $\mathfrak{G}$ satisfies, it can be easily verified that all axioms in **VCn** are valid in $\mathfrak{G}$, and $\mathfrak{G}$ preserves validity for the rule RCEC. But CA is not valid in $\mathfrak{G}$, since $g(0, A \cup B) = \{1, 2, 3\} \not\subseteq \{1, 3\} = g(0, A) \cup g(0, B)$. Therefore $\nvDash_{\mathbf{Vn}}$ CA. $\qquad \square$

Corollary 3.2 $\nvDash_{\mathbf{Vn}}$ CA [4]

Now we show that by replacing MOD$'$ with CA in the corresponding systems, Nute's axiomatizations can be amended. Let

$$\mathbf{Va} = \langle \mathrm{PC}, \mathrm{ID}, \mathrm{CSO}, \mathrm{DAE}; \mathrm{RCK} \rangle$$
$$\mathbf{Vb} = \langle \mathrm{PC}, \mathrm{ID}, \mathrm{MOD}', \mathrm{PIE}; \mathrm{RCK}, \mathrm{RE} \rangle$$
$$\mathbf{Vc} = \langle \mathrm{PC}, \mathrm{ID}, \mathrm{CM}, \mathrm{CC}, \mathrm{CV}, \mathrm{CA}, \mathrm{CSO}; \mathrm{RCEC} \rangle$$
$$\mathbf{VCa} = \langle \mathrm{PC}, \mathrm{ID}, \mathrm{CSO}, \mathrm{DAE}, \mathrm{CMP}, \mathrm{CS}; \mathrm{RCK} \rangle$$
$$\mathbf{VCb} = \langle \mathrm{PC}, \mathrm{ID}, \mathrm{MOD}', \mathrm{PIE}, \mathrm{CMP}, \mathrm{CS}; \mathrm{RCK}, \mathrm{RE} \rangle$$
$$\mathbf{VCc} = \langle \mathrm{PC}, \mathrm{ID}, \mathrm{CM}, \mathrm{CC}, \mathrm{CV}, \mathrm{CA}, \mathrm{CSO}, \mathrm{CMP}, \mathrm{CS}; \mathrm{RCEC} \rangle,$$

where **Va** and **VCa** are Lewis' first axiomatizations of **V** and **VC**, respectively; **Vb** and **VCb** are his second axiomatizations; **Vc** and **VCc** are amendments of Nute's systems for **V** and **VC**, respectively. To prove that these amendments are equivalent to Lewis' original systems, it suffices to prove that **Vc** is equivalent to **Va** or **Vb**. Since **Va** = **Vb**, if suffices to show that **Vc** ⊇ **Va** and **Vb** ⊇ **Vc**.

Proposition 3.3 **Vc** = **Va** = **Vb**.

Proof. First, we show that **Vc** ⊇ **Va**. For simplification of proofs, we will first prove that RCM, RCE, RCN, and RCEA are derivable in **Vc**.

For RCM:

---

[4] Nute also gave the axiomatization **VWn** = $\langle \mathrm{PC}, \mathrm{ID}, \mathrm{CV}, \mathrm{MOD}', \mathrm{CSO}, \mathrm{CMP}; \mathrm{RCEC}, \mathrm{RCK} \rangle$ for Lewis' system **VW**. So neither is CA derivable from **VWn**. The reason why CA is missing from Nute's axiomatization is not clear, since no explicit proof of completeness of these systems was given in his writings. We guess the reason may be that CA is derivable in his axiomatization of **C2**.

(1) $\varphi \to \psi$	Assumption
(2) $\varphi \wedge \psi \leftrightarrow \varphi$	(1), PC
(3) $(\chi > \varphi \wedge \psi) \leftrightarrow (\chi > \varphi)$	(2), RCEC
(4) $(\chi > \varphi \wedge \psi) \to (\chi > \psi)$	CM, PC
(5) $(\chi > \varphi) \to (\chi > \psi)$	(3), (4), PC

For RCE:

(1) $\varphi \to \psi$	Assumption
(2) $(\varphi > \varphi) \to (\varphi > \psi)$	(1), RCM
(3) $\varphi > \varphi$	ID
(4) $\varphi > \psi$	(2), (3), PC

For RCN:

(1) ψ	Assumption
(2) $\varphi \to \psi$	(1), PC
(3) $\varphi > \psi$	(2), RCE

For RCEA:

(1) $\varphi \leftrightarrow \psi$	Assumption
(2) $\varphi \to \psi, \psi \to \varphi$	(1), PC
(3) $\varphi > \psi, \psi > \varphi$	(2), RCE
(4) $(\varphi > \chi) \leftrightarrow (\psi > \chi)$	(3), CSO, PC

Now we prove that RCK is derivable in **Vc**. The case for $n = 0$ is just RCN. The case for $n = 1$ is just RCM. It remains to prove the case for $n = 2$. The case for $n > 2$ can be obtained similarly.

(1) $\psi_1 \wedge \psi_2 \to \psi$	Assumption
(2) $(\varphi > \psi_1 \wedge \psi_2) \to (\varphi > \psi)$	(1), RCM
(3) $(\varphi > \psi_1) \wedge (\varphi > \psi_2) \to (\varphi > \psi_1 \wedge \psi_2)$	CC
(4) $(\varphi > \psi_1) \wedge (\varphi > \psi_2) \to (\varphi > \psi)$	(2), (3), PC

Next we prove that DAE is derivable in **Vc**. By CA, it suffices to prove $(\varphi \vee \psi > \varphi) \vee (\varphi \vee \psi > \psi) \vee ((\varphi \vee \psi > \chi) \to (\varphi > \chi) \wedge (\psi > \chi))$.

(1) $(\varphi \vee \psi > \chi) \wedge \neg(\varphi \vee \psi > \neg(\neg\varphi \vee \psi)) \to ((\varphi \vee \psi) \wedge (\neg\varphi \vee \psi) > \chi)$	CV
(2) $(\varphi \vee \psi) \wedge (\neg\varphi \vee \psi) \leftrightarrow \psi$	PC
(3) $(\varphi \vee \psi > \chi) \wedge \neg(\varphi \vee \psi > \neg(\neg\varphi \vee \psi)) \to (\psi > \chi)$	(1), (2), RCEA, PC
(4) $(\varphi \vee \psi > \chi) \wedge \neg(\varphi \vee \psi > \neg(\varphi \vee \neg\psi)) \to ((\varphi \vee \psi) \wedge (\varphi \vee \neg\psi) > \chi)$	CV
(5) $(\varphi \vee \psi) \wedge (\varphi \vee \neg\psi) \leftrightarrow \varphi$	PC
(6) $(\varphi \vee \psi > \chi) \wedge \neg(\varphi \vee \psi > \neg(\varphi \vee \neg\psi)) \to (\varphi > \chi)$	(4), (5), RCEA, PC
(7) $\neg(\neg\varphi \vee \psi) \to \varphi$	PC

(8) $(\varphi \vee \psi > \neg(\neg\varphi \vee \psi)) \rightarrow (\varphi \vee \psi > \varphi)$ (7), RCM

(9) $\neg(\varphi \vee \psi > \varphi) \rightarrow \neg(\varphi \vee \psi > \neg(\neg\varphi \vee \psi))$ (8), PC

(10) $\neg(\varphi \vee \neg\psi) \rightarrow \psi$ PC

(11) $(\varphi \vee \psi > \neg(\varphi \vee \neg\psi)) \rightarrow (\varphi \vee \psi > \psi)$ (10), RCM

(12) $\neg(\varphi \vee \psi > \psi) \rightarrow \neg(\varphi \vee \psi > \neg(\varphi \vee \neg\psi))$ (11), PC

(13) $\neg(\varphi \vee \psi > \varphi) \wedge \neg(\varphi \vee \psi > \psi) \wedge (\varphi \vee \psi > \chi) \rightarrow (\varphi > \chi) \wedge (\psi > \chi)$ (3), (6),
     (9), (12), PC

(14) $(\varphi \vee \psi > \varphi) \vee (\varphi \vee \psi > \psi) \vee ((\varphi \vee \psi > \chi) \rightarrow (\varphi > \chi) \wedge (\psi > \chi))$ (13), PC

This completes the proof of **Vc** $\supseteq$ **Va**.

Now we prove **Vb** $\supseteq$ **Vc**. The derivation of CC and CM is straightforward using RCK. The rule RCEC is a special case of RE. It remains to show that CA, CV, and CSO are derivable in **Vb**.

For CV:

(1) $\neg(\varphi > \neg\psi) \wedge (\varphi > (\psi \rightarrow \chi)) \rightarrow (\varphi \wedge \psi > \chi)$ PIE, PC

(2) $\chi \rightarrow (\psi \rightarrow \chi)$ PC

(3) $(\varphi > \chi) \rightarrow (\varphi > (\psi \rightarrow \chi))$ (2), RCK

(4) $(\varphi > \chi) \wedge \neg(\varphi > \neg\psi) \rightarrow (\varphi \wedge \psi > \chi)$ (1), (3), PC

For CSO: Let $\alpha = \varphi > \neg\psi$, $\beta = \psi > \neg\varphi$. By PC, it suffices to prove

(c) $\neg\alpha \wedge \neg\beta \wedge (\varphi > \psi) \wedge (\psi > \varphi) \rightarrow ((\varphi > \chi) \leftrightarrow (\psi > \chi))$,

(d) $\alpha \wedge (\varphi > \psi) \wedge (\psi > \varphi) \rightarrow ((\varphi > \chi) \leftrightarrow (\psi > \chi))$, and

(e) $\beta \wedge (\varphi > \psi) \wedge (\psi > \varphi) \rightarrow ((\varphi > \chi) \leftrightarrow (\psi > \chi))$.

For (c):

(1) $\neg\alpha \rightarrow ((\varphi \wedge \psi > \chi) \leftrightarrow (\varphi > (\psi \rightarrow \chi)))$ PIE

(2) $\psi \wedge (\psi \rightarrow \chi) \rightarrow \chi$ PC

(3) $(\varphi > \psi) \wedge (\varphi > (\psi \rightarrow \chi)) \rightarrow (\varphi > \chi)$ (2), RCK

(4) $\chi \rightarrow (\psi \rightarrow \chi)$ PC

(5) $(\varphi > \chi) \rightarrow (\varphi > (\psi \rightarrow \chi))$ (4), RCK

(6) $\neg\alpha \wedge (\varphi > \psi) \rightarrow ((\varphi > \chi) \leftrightarrow (\varphi \wedge \psi > \chi))$ (1), (3), (5), PC

(7) $\neg\beta \wedge (\psi > \varphi) \rightarrow ((\psi > \chi) \leftrightarrow (\varphi \wedge \psi > \chi))$ analogous to (1)–(6)

(8) $\neg\alpha \wedge \neg\beta \wedge (\varphi > \psi) \wedge (\psi > \varphi) \rightarrow ((\varphi > \chi) \leftrightarrow (\psi > \chi))$ (6), (7), PC

For (d):

(1) $\neg\psi \wedge \psi \rightarrow \chi$ PC

(2) $\alpha \wedge (\varphi > \psi) \rightarrow (\varphi > \chi)$ (1), RCK

(3) $\neg\psi \wedge \psi \rightarrow \neg\varphi$ PC

(4) $\alpha \wedge (\varphi > \psi) \rightarrow (\varphi > \neg\varphi)$ (3), RCK

(5) $(\varphi > \neg\varphi) \rightarrow (\psi > \neg\varphi)$ MOD

(6) $\alpha \wedge (\varphi > \psi) \rightarrow (\psi > \neg\varphi)$ $\hfill$ (4), (5), PC

(7) $\alpha \wedge (\varphi > \psi) \wedge (\psi > \varphi) \rightarrow (\psi > \varphi \wedge \neg\varphi)$ $\hfill$ (6), RCK, PC

(8) $\varphi \wedge \neg\varphi \rightarrow \chi$ $\hfill$ PC

(9) $\alpha \wedge (\varphi > \psi) \wedge (\psi > \varphi) \rightarrow (\psi > \chi)$ $\hfill$ (7), (8), RCK, PC

(10) $\alpha \wedge (\varphi > \psi) \wedge (\psi > \varphi) \rightarrow ((\varphi > \chi) \leftrightarrow (\psi > \chi))$ $\hfill$ (2), (9), PC

Note that in the above derivation, we use MOD instead of MOD', so that we can dispense with RE. If MOD' is used instead, then the derivation is longer, with an additional line of transforming MOD' to MOD, using RE.

(e) can be proved analogously to (d).

For CA: Let $\alpha = \varphi \vee \psi > \neg\varphi$, $\beta = \varphi \vee \psi > \neg\psi$. It suffices to prove

(f) $\neg\alpha \wedge \neg\beta \wedge (\varphi > \chi) \wedge (\psi > \chi) \rightarrow (\varphi \vee \psi > \chi)$,

(g) $\alpha \wedge (\varphi > \chi) \wedge (\psi > \chi) \rightarrow (\varphi \vee \psi > \chi)$, and

(h) $\beta \wedge (\varphi > \chi) \wedge (\psi > \chi) \rightarrow (\varphi \vee \psi > \chi)$.

For (f):

(1) $\neg\alpha \wedge ((\varphi \vee \psi) \wedge \varphi > \chi) \rightarrow (\varphi \vee \psi > (\varphi \rightarrow \chi))$ $\hfill$ PIE, PC

(2) $(\varphi \vee \psi) \wedge \varphi \leftrightarrow \varphi$ $\hfill$ PC

(3) $\neg\alpha \wedge (\varphi > \chi) \rightarrow (\varphi \vee \psi > (\varphi \rightarrow \chi))$ $\hfill$ (1), (2), RE

(4) $\neg\beta \wedge (\psi > \chi) \rightarrow (\varphi \vee \psi > (\psi \rightarrow \chi))$ $\hfill$ analogous to (1)–(3)

(5) $\varphi \vee \psi > \varphi \vee \psi$ $\hfill$ ID

(6) $(\varphi \vee \psi) \wedge (\varphi \rightarrow \chi) \wedge (\psi \rightarrow \chi) \rightarrow \chi$ $\hfill$ PC

(7) $(\varphi \vee \psi > (\varphi \rightarrow \chi)) \wedge (\varphi \vee \chi > (\psi \rightarrow \chi)) \rightarrow (\varphi \vee \psi > \chi)$(5), (6), RCK, PC

(8) $\neg\alpha \wedge \neg\beta \wedge (\varphi > \chi) \wedge (\psi > \chi) \rightarrow (\varphi \vee \psi > \chi)$ $\hfill$ (3), (4), (7), PC

For (g):

(1) $(\varphi \vee \psi) \wedge \neg\varphi \rightarrow \psi$ $\hfill$ PC

(2) $\varphi \vee \psi > \varphi \vee \psi$ $\hfill$ ID

(3) $\alpha \rightarrow (\varphi \vee \psi > \psi)$ $\hfill$ (1), (2), RCK, PC

(4) $\psi > \varphi \vee \psi$ $\hfill$ PC, RCK, ID

(5) $\alpha \wedge (\psi > \chi) \rightarrow (\varphi \vee \psi > \chi)$ $\hfill$ (3), (4), CSO

(6) $\alpha \wedge (\varphi > \chi) \wedge (\psi > \chi) \rightarrow (\varphi \vee \psi > \chi)$ $\hfill$ (5), PC

(h) can be prove analogously to (g).

This completes the proof of **Vb** $\supseteq$ **Vc**. $\hfill$ $\square$

Corollary 3.4 **VCc** $=$ **VCa** $=$ **VCb**.

4 New Axiomatizations of Lewis' Conditional Logics

We propose the following new axiomatizations of Lewis' conditional logics, which are denoted by $\mathbf{V}'$ and $\mathbf{VC}'$, respectively.

$$\mathbf{V}' = \langle PC, ID, CM, CA, CV, AC, RT; RCEC \rangle$$
$$\mathbf{VC}' = \langle PC, ID, CM, CA, CV, AC, RT, CMP, CS; RCEC \rangle$$

Both systems replace the axiom CSO by the axioms AC and RT in $\mathbf{Vc}$ and $\mathbf{VCc}$, respectively. Meanwhile, CC is omitted, since it is derivable from other axioms and rules. We will prove that the new axiomatizations are equivalent to Lewis' original ones. By Proposition 3.3 and Corollary 3.4, it suffices to prove that $\mathbf{V}'$ is equivalent to $\mathbf{Vc}$.

Proposition 4.1 $\mathbf{V}' = \mathbf{Vc}$.

Proof. First, we show that $\mathbf{Vc} \supseteq \mathbf{V}'$, i.e. AC and RT are derivable in $\mathbf{Vc}$.
For AC:

(1) $(\varphi > \varphi) \wedge (\varphi > \psi) \to (\varphi > \varphi \wedge \psi)$ CC
(2) $\varphi > \varphi$ ID
(3) $(\varphi > \psi) \to (\varphi > \varphi \wedge \psi)$ (1), (2), PC
(4) $\varphi \wedge \psi \to \varphi$ PC
(5) $\varphi \wedge \psi > \varphi$ (4), RCE
(6) $(\varphi > \psi) \to (\varphi > \varphi \wedge \psi) \wedge (\varphi \wedge \psi > \varphi)$ (3), (5), PC
(7) $(\varphi > \varphi \wedge \psi) \wedge (\varphi \wedge \psi > \varphi) \to ((\varphi > \chi) \leftrightarrow (\varphi \wedge \psi > \chi))$ CSO
(8) $(\varphi > \psi) \wedge (\varphi > \chi) \to (\varphi \wedge \psi > \chi)$ (6), (7), PC

For RT:

(1) $\psi \wedge \varphi \to \varphi$ PC
(2) $\psi \wedge \varphi > \varphi$ (1), RCE
(3) $\varphi > \varphi$ ID
(4) $(\varphi > \psi) \to (\varphi > \psi \wedge \varphi)$ (3), CC, PC
(5) $(\varphi > \psi) \to (\varphi > \psi \wedge \varphi) \wedge (\psi \wedge \varphi > \varphi)$ (2), (4), PC
(6) $(\varphi > \psi \wedge \varphi) \wedge (\psi \wedge \varphi > \varphi) \to ((\varphi > \chi) \leftrightarrow (\psi \wedge \varphi > \chi))$ CSO
(7) $(\varphi > \psi) \wedge (\psi \wedge \varphi > \chi) \to (\varphi > \chi)$ (5), (6), PC

Then we show that $\mathbf{V}' \supseteq \mathbf{Vc}$.
For CSO:

(1) $(\varphi > \psi) \wedge (\varphi > \chi) \to (\varphi \wedge \psi > \chi)$ AC
(2) $(\psi > \varphi) \wedge (\varphi \wedge \psi > \chi) \to (\psi > \chi)$ RT
(3) $(\varphi > \psi) \wedge (\psi > \varphi) \wedge (\varphi > \chi) \to (\psi > \chi)$ (1), (2), PC
(4) $(\varphi > \psi) \wedge (\psi > \varphi) \wedge (\psi > \chi) \to (\varphi > \chi)$ analogous to (1)–(3)

(5) $(\varphi > \psi) \wedge (\psi > \varphi) \rightarrow ((\varphi > \chi) \leftrightarrow (\psi > \chi))$ (3), (4), PC

To prove CC, note that we have proved that RCE can be obtained from PC, ID, CM, and RCEC in the proof of Proposition 3.3. Since RCEA follows from RCE and CSO, we also have RCEA in **V'**. Now we have the following derivation for CC:

(1) $\varphi \wedge \psi \wedge \chi > \varphi \wedge \psi \wedge \chi$ ID

(2) $\varphi \wedge \psi \wedge \chi > \psi \wedge \chi$ (1), CM, PC

(3) $\varphi \wedge \psi \wedge \chi \leftrightarrow \chi \wedge \varphi \wedge \psi$ PC

(4) $\chi \wedge \varphi \wedge \psi > \psi \wedge \chi$ (2), (3), RCEA, PC

(5) $(\varphi > \psi) \wedge (\varphi > \chi) \rightarrow (\varphi \wedge \psi > \chi)$ AC

(6) $(\varphi > \psi) \wedge (\varphi > \chi) \rightarrow (\varphi \wedge \psi > \psi \wedge \chi)$ (4), (5), RT, PC

(7) $\varphi \wedge \psi \leftrightarrow \psi \wedge \varphi$ PC

(8) $(\varphi \wedge \psi > \psi \wedge \chi) \rightarrow (\psi \wedge \varphi > \psi \wedge \chi)$ (7), RCEA

(9) $(\varphi > \psi) \wedge (\psi \wedge \varphi > \psi \wedge \chi) \rightarrow (\varphi > \psi \wedge \chi)$ RT

(10) $(\varphi > \psi) \wedge (\varphi > \chi) \rightarrow (\varphi > \psi \wedge \chi)$ (6), (8), (9), PC

□

Corollary 4.2 VC' = VCc.

The axiom CSO was criticized by Gabbay [5]. One may be inclined to abandon it directly. However, the above new systems show that CSO can be recovered from AC and RT. It should be easy to notice that AC and RT correspond to cautious monotonicity and cautious cut (a.k.a. cumulative transitivity) in non-monotonic logics. Both cautious monotonicity and cautious cut are regarded as the minimal requirements for nonmonotonic consequences. If AC and RT are also taken to be minimal for conditional logics, then the above proof shows that CSO is inevitable in conditional logics. If CSO is inevitable, then RCEA is also inevitable, since it follows from CSO and the very intuitive axiom RCE. The new axiomatization indicates that it is difficult to construct nonclassical conditional logics for characterizing default conditionals. It also leads us to a puzzle about the controversial axiom SDA, which is the converse of CA.

5   A Resolution of a Puzzle about SDA

The axiom SDA suggests that conditionals with disjunctive antecedents have conjunctive reading. For example, when I say that if John or Mary comes to my party, I'll be happy, it is reasonable to conclude that if John comes to my party I'll be happy, and if Mary comes to my party I'll be happy. But if SDA is contained in any conditional logic with the rule RCEA, the so called fallacy of strengthening the antecedent which is rejected in all conditional logics will be recovered. This can be shown by the following simple derivation:

(1) $\varphi \leftrightarrow (\varphi \vee (\varphi \wedge \psi))$ PC

(2) $(\varphi \vee (\varphi \wedge \psi) > \chi) \rightarrow \varphi \wedge \psi > \chi$ SDA, PC

(3) $(\varphi > \chi) \to (\varphi \wedge \psi > \chi)$ (1), (2), RCEA, PC

There are mainly three approaches to solving this puzzle. The first approach, adopted in [10,11,15,8], is to abandon SDA and apply something other than logic such as translation lore to account for the intuitive validity of SDA. The second approach, adopted in [12,13,14], is to keep SDA while giving up the rule RCEA by developing nonclassical conditional logics. As we have seen in Section 4, this means that some other intuitively reasonable axioms such as AC or RT have to be abandoned too. In [4], both the first two approaches were suggested. The third approach, adopted in [1,6,18], is to give nonclassical interpretations for disjunction, so that the disjunctive antecedents in conditionals have conjunctive reading. All the approaches are somewhat ad hoc, in the sense that conditionals with disjunctive antecedents are treated as special and different from other conditionals.

It has been noticed that SDA has counterexamples in both counterfactual and indicative conditionals. The following is one for counterfactuals given in [11]:

(1) If Spain fought on the Axis side or fought on the Allied side, it would fight on the Axis side.

(2) If Spain fought on the Allied side, it would fight on the Axis side.

By SDA, (1) implies (2). But obviously (2) is false even if (1) is true. A similar counterexample for indicative conditionals was given in [3]:

(3) If Ivan is playing tennis or playing baseball, then he is playing baseball.

(4) If Ivan is playing tennis, then he is playing baseball.

By SDA, (3) implies (4). But we can have (3) true and (4) false. Both counterexamples have the following form: $\varphi \vee \psi > \varphi$ is true but $\psi > \varphi$ false. As far as we know, no other forms of counterexamples of SDA have been discovered. Considering that SDA has only counterexamples of such special forms, one can not resist keeping SDA while explaining away such counterexamples by attributing them as abnormal uses of conditionals with disjunctive antecedents. But we still face the conflict between SDA and RCEA. Remarkably, one of Lewis' axioms for conditional logics, namely the old-fashioned axiom DAE, which has been neglected for a long time, can perfectly account for both the intuitive validity of SDA and its counterexamples! The axiom DAE says that either $\varphi \vee \psi > \varphi$ is true, or $\varphi \vee \psi > \psi$ is true, or $(\varphi \vee \psi > \chi)$ is logically equivalent to $(\varphi > \chi) \wedge (\psi > \chi)$. From DAE it follows that

$$\neg(\varphi \vee \psi > \varphi) \wedge \neg(\varphi \vee \psi > \psi) \to \text{SDA},$$

which is weaker than SDA. But it is not too weak, since as long as we exclude the cases when the disjunctive antecedent conditionally implies one of its disjuncts, which are exactly the counterexamples for SDA we have found, SDA is obtained. We think this resolution of the puzzle around SDA is better than previous ones, since we can dispense with any special treatments of the conditionals with disjunctive antecedents. It is a big surprise that Lewis himself did not discover this simple solution, even though he had published a note [8] about SDA some years after he proposed the axiom DAE in [7].

References

[1] Alonso-Ovalle, L., "Disjunction in Alternative Semantics," CreateSpace Independent Publishing Platform, 2010.

[2] Arló Costa, H., *The logic of conditionals*, in: Edward N. Zalta, editor, *The Stanford Encyclopedia of Philosophy (Summer 2014 Edition)*, 2014 .

[3] Carlstrom, I. F. and C. S. Hill, *The Logic of Conditionals by Ernest W. Adams*, Philosophy of Science **45** (1978), pp. 155–158.

[4] Fine, K., *Normal forms in modal logic.*, Notre Dame Journal of Formal Logic **16** (1975), pp. 229–237.

[5] Gabbay, D. M., *A general theory of the conditional in terms of a ternary operator*, Theoria **38** (1972), pp. 97–104.

[6] Klinedinst, N. W., "Plurality and Possibility," Ph.D. thesis, University of California at Los Angeles (2007).

[7] Lewis, D., *Completeness and Decidability of Three Logics of Counterfactual Conditionals*, Theoria **37** (1971), pp. 74–85.

[8] Lewis, D., *Possible-World Semantics for Counterfactual Logics: A Rejoinder*, Journal of Philosophical Logic **6** (1977), pp. 359–363.

[9] Lewis, D. K., *Counterfactuals and Comparative Possibility*, Journal of Philosophical Logic **2** (1973), pp. 418–446.

[10] Loewer, B., *Counterfactuals with Disjunctive Antecedents*, The Journal of Philosophy **73** (1976), pp. 531–537.

[11] McKay, T. and P. van Inwagen, *Counterfactuals with Disjunctive Antecedents*, Philosophical Studies **31** (1977), pp. 353–356.

[12] Nute, D., *Counterfactuals and the Similarity of Worlds*, Journal of Philosophy **72** (1975), pp. 773–778.

[13] Nute, D., *Simplification and Substitution of Counterfactual Antecedents*, Philosophia **2** (1978), pp. 317–325.

[14] Nute, D., *Conversational Scorekeeping and Conditionals*, Journal of Philosophical Logic **9** (1980), pp. 153–166.

[15] Nute, D., "Topics in Conditional Logic," Reidel, 1980.

[16] Nute, D., *Conditional Logic*, in: F. Guenthner and D. Gabbay, editors, *Handbook of Philosophical Logic, Vol.II*, Springer, Dordrecht, 1984 pp. 387–439.

[17] Nute, D. and C. B. Cross, *Conditional Logic*, in: D. Gabbay, editor, *Handbook of Philosophical Logic, Vol.4*, D. Reidel, Dordrecht, 2001 pp. 1–98.

[18] Paoli, F., *A Paraconsistent and Substructural Conditional Logic*, in: K. Tanaka, F. Berto, E. Mares and F. Paoli, editors, *Paraconsistency: Logic and Applications*, Springer, 2012 pp. 173–198.

[19] Pozzato, G. L., "Conditional and Preferential Logic," IOS Press, 2010.

Using ATS to Model Control Argumentation in Multi-agent Settings (Extended Abstract)

Muyun Shao

ZLAIRE
Zhejiang University

Beishui Liao

ZLAIRE
Zhejiang University

Abstract

Control argumentation frameworks describe meaningful models for an agent to make decisions in an unpredictable but foreseeable environment that is represented by a set of uncertain arguments. But in a multi-agent setting they fail to capture both coalition formation and interactions among a set of agents in an unforeseeable environment. To study this problem, we propose a model of multi-agent control game and study how agents adjust their strategies and form coalitions in reaction to unforeseeable changes of the environment.

Keywords: Control argumentation, alternating transition system, coalition formation, argument enforcement

1 Introduction

Formal argumentation offers a natural and easily understood form of non-monotonic reasoning, and has been applied to various domains such as legal reasoning and coalition formation [2,3,4,9]. It starts with abstract argumentation frameworks proposed by Dung [6], and then several extensions based on it including structured argumentation frameworks, bipolar argumentation frameworks and probabilistic argumentation frameworks, etc. As a new family of formal argumentation, control argumentation frameworks [5] aim to reach certain state (acceptance/rejection of particular arguments to be ensured) regardless of unpredictable threats they may face in a dynamic environment represented by a set of uncertain arguments. In the majority of extended abstract argumentation frameworks such as structured argumentation frameworks [7], frameworks are assumed to be fixed, without uncertainty about the existence of arguments. Control argumentation frameworks (CAFs) relax this assumption, allowing different possible changes in the frameworks including the addition and removal of arguments and/or attacks. These changes may affect the status of arguments in an argumentation system. The main theme of CAFs is to study how to maintain desired status of particular arguments which can resist unpredictable changes of the uncertain arguments.

Since the existing theories of CAFs only focus on enforcing the status of some arguments, rather than describe how agents interact with each other in an unforeseeable environment, they may not be directly applicable to multi-agent game settings. In a CAF, agents are assumed to know the whole framework. Even some arguments are uncertain, any change of arguments may be unpredictable but foreseeable. While in reality agents may encounter some problems which may not be foreseeable. For instance, a driver may find his car stopped suddenly without any foreseeable problem, or a representative may realize that the opponent has already known his bottom line in the middle of the negotiation without any previous evidence. In these cases agents may adjust his/her model of the environment as well as his/her strategy according to information provided by the environment. There are also some other cases in which the agent may not be able to ensure certain status of particular arguments and may need help from others. Take the prisoner dilemma as an example, one prisoner is unable to ensure the best situation unless he collaborates with the other one. CAFs fail to capture these intuitions and naturally give rise to the following research question:

> How agents adjust their beliefs and strategies and form coalitions in reaction to unforeseeable changes of the environment in the setting of control argumentation?

To study this problem, we propose a method based on alternating transition system, and exploit a language and its semantics based on the existing theory of alternating-time temporal logic to represent control propositions and coalition formation in argumentation.

The structure of this paper is organized as follows. In the next section, we will give a brief introduction of some basic notions of CAFs and alternating transition system. Then, in section 3, we introduce the basic idea of our method by defining a control game structure. Finally, we conclude the paper with a final remark.

2   Preliminaries

2.1   Control Argumentation Frameworks

A control argumentation framework [5] is a triple $CAF = (C, F, U)$ which describes a model of environment including arguments controlled by the agent (the control part C), arguments which are certain but not controlled (the fixed part F), and uncertain arguments (the uncertain part U). The goal is to find a strategy, namely a subset of the arguments controlled by the agent, which ensures certain status of particular arguments in all possible cases. If such status is ensured, we say that the status is controlled by the strategy. In the control game structure introduced in the next section, we use a control proposition to represent the controlled status of a certain argument with respect to a state, for instance $acc(\alpha)$ denotes the acceptance of an argument α.

2.2 Alternating Transition System

An alternating transition system (ATS) [1] is a tuple $S = (\Pi, \Sigma, Q, \pi, \delta)$ with the following components: Π is a set of propositions. Σ is a set of agents. Q is a set of states and q_0 is the initial state. $\pi : Q \to 2^\Pi$ maps each state to the set of propositions that are true in the state. $\delta : Q \times \Sigma \to 2^{2^Q}$ maps a state and an agent to a non-empty set of choices, where each choice is a set of possible next state.

3 Control Game Structure

In this section we will give an introduction of the multi-agent control game structure. In order to form a multi-agent control game which is capable of representing coalition formations and modifications of agents' beliefs and strategies in the setting of control argumentation, we propose a method combining ATS and control argumentation introduced in the preliminaries to build a modified version of ATS. For components mentioned in the preliminaries, i.e. $\Pi, \Sigma, Q, \pi, \delta$, we do not modify them except that we let Π be the set of all control propositions. Besides that we propose several new components in our game structure to represent agents' beliefs and strategies, including α representing agents' possible strategies in a given state, CAF representing agents' models of the environment (the $CAFs$) and an updating function upd, of which the idea is inspired by [8], describing adjustments of agents' models. We give a formal definition of these modifications in Definition 3.1.

Definition 3.1 (Game structure) A Multi-agent Control Game Structure $(MCGS)$ is a tuple $S = (\Pi, \Sigma, Q, \pi, \delta, \alpha, CAF, upd)$ where

- $\alpha : Q \times \Sigma \to N$ (where N is the set of natural numbers) is a function which gives a number to each available action for an agent $i \in \Sigma$ at a state $q \in Q$. In a control game structure, actions of agents are simply strategies. At each state q, we denote the set of joint strategies for all agents in Σ by $\Sigma(q)$.

- $\delta : Q \times \Sigma(q) \to Q$ is the transition function where $\delta(q, m)$ is the next state from q if players execute the action $m \in \Sigma(q)$.

- CAF is the set of all possible control argumentation frameworks and CAF_0 is the actual dynamic environment in which we compute control propositions.

- $upd : CAF \times \Sigma(q) \to CAF$ is a function used to update agents' models of the environment where $upd(CAF_i, m)$ is the new model updated from a previous model CAF_i given that a joint action $m \in \Sigma(q)$ is executed.

The multi-agent control game structure alone is not sufficient to study the research question mentioned above. We still need to define a language which is capable of representing control propositions in the game structure. The way we define the language depends on what properties of control argumentation we are interested in. In this paper we pay attention to three types of them, that are (1)whether certain status of an argument is controlled at a state, (2)whether a control proposition can be the semantic consequence of another control proposition (independent of states) and (3)whether a coalition can control certain status of a particular argument. The corresponding three types of control propositions are called normal control propositions, conditional control propositions and coalitional control propositions. We give a formal definition of the language in Definition 3.2 for better understanding.

Definition 3.2 (Syntax and Semantics) The language of $MCGS$ is defined as follows:

$$p \in \Pi | \neg \phi | \phi \wedge \psi | \phi \rightarrow \psi | [C] \phi$$

The truth condition of formulas in MCGS is defined as follows:

- $q \vDash p$ iff $p \in \pi(q)$.
- $q \vDash \neg \phi$ iff $q \nvDash \phi$.
- $q \vDash \phi \wedge \psi$ iff $q \vDash \phi$ and $q \vDash \psi$.
- $q \vDash \phi \rightarrow \psi$ iff for all states $q' \in Q$, if $q' \vDash \phi$ then $q' \vDash \psi$.
- $q \vDash [C] \phi$ iff there exists a set of agents $C \subseteq \Sigma$ and a joint action a_c of C such that for any $m \in \Sigma(q)$, if $a_c \subseteq m$ then $\delta(q, m) \vDash \phi$.

For any $\mathcal{A} \subseteq \Pi$, we write $q \vDash \mathcal{A}$ for $q \vDash \bigwedge_{a \in \mathcal{A}} a$

By virtue of the game structure and the language, the game model is capable of representing control propositions in multi-agent settings. What left to be discussed is how agents evaluate different control strategies which may have different outcomes, namely the payoffs of the strategies. In this paper we use argumentation goals to set foundations for evaluating strategies, of which the idea is in correspondence with the basic idea of control argumentation, i.e. whether a set of desired status of arguments is ensured. Considering that some other works [2,4] give a preorder to measure outcomes, we also define a preorder on outcomes based on to what extent they satisfy the argumentation goals.

Definition 3.3 (Argumentation goals and weak preference relation). The argumentation goals of agent i is a set of propositional variables $G_i \subseteq \Pi$ which denotes the desired status of particular arguments. For each agent i, $\geqslant_i$ is a partial order on Q which is reflexive, transitive and asymmetric. $q \geqslant_i q'$ iff for all $\mathcal{A} \subseteq G_i$, if $q' \models \mathcal{A}$, then $q \vDash \mathcal{A}$.

4   Final Remark

In this paper, we present a multi-agent control game structure to model (1) agents' interaction, (2) adjustments of their beliefs and strategies and (3) coalitional controllability in multi-agent settings. In future work, there are two topics we are interested in. The first topic is the details of *upd* function. In [8] the authors presented a reasonable version of *upd* function in the setting of abstract argumentation. But in the setting of control argumentation, an agent needs to distinguish between the fixed arguments and arguments controlled by other agents. We may not simply add new arguments into agents' models, but label them as fixed arguments or arguments controlled by a particular agent by virtue of some rational disciplines.

The second topic is, given a particular argument, how to find minimal subsets of controlled arguments (w.r.t set inclusion), such that a particular control configuration of these arguments controls the desired status of that argument. This topic is familiar with a topic in dynamics of argumentation called enforcement. The difference is that in our setting there are more restrictions. For instance, there is no reason to add/remove the facts (the fixed arguments) and their attack relations, as well as actions of other agents (the arguments controlled by other agents). An algorithm of such procedure may give insights in modelling coalition formation in the control game structure.

References

[1] Alur, R., T. A. Henzinger and O. Kupferman, *Alternating-time temporal logic*, Journal of the ACM (JACM) (2002), pp. 672–713.

[2] Amgoud, L., *An argumentation-based model for reasoning about coalition structures.*, in: *International Workshop on Argumentation in Multi-Agent Systems*, Springer, 2005, pp. 217–228.

[3] Amgoud, L., *Towards a formal model for task allocation via coalition formation*, in: *Proceedings of the fourth international joint conference on Autonomous agents and multiagent systems*, 2005, pp. 1185–1186.

[4] Bulling, N., J. Dix and C. I. Chesnevar, *Modelling coalitions: Atl+ argumentation.*, in: *AAMAS (2)*, 2008, pp. 681–688.

[5] Dimopoulos, Y., J.-G. Mailly and P. Moraitis, *Control argumentation frameworks*, in: *Proceedings of the AAAI Conference on Artificial Intelligence*, 1, 2018.

[6] Dung, P. M., *On the acceptability of arguments and its fundamental role in nonmonotonic reasoning, logic programming and n-person games*, Artificial intelligence **77** (1995), pp. 321–357.

[7] Modgil, S. and H. Prakken, *The aspic+ framework for structured argumentation: a tutorial*, Argument & Computation **5** (2014), pp. 31–62.

[8] Rienstra, T., M. Thimm and N. Oren, *Opponent models with uncertainty for strategic argumentation*, in: *Twenty-Third International Joint Conference on Artificial Intelligence*, 2013.

[9] Roth, B., R. Riveret, A. Rotolo and G. Governatori, *Strategic argumentation: a game theoretical investigation*, in: *Proceedings of the 11th international conference on artificial intelligence and law*, 2007, pp. 81–90.